THE ULTIMATE
AIR FRYER
COOKBOOK

The paper in this printing meets the requirements of the ANSI Standard Z39.48-1992.

While every care has been taken in compiling the recipes for this book, the publisher, Cogin, Inc., or any other person who has been involved in working on this publication assumes no responsibility or liability for any errors or omissions, inadvertent or not, that may be found in the recipes or text, nor for any problems or damages that may arise as a result of preparing these recipes.

If food allergies or dietary restrictions are a concern, it is recommended that you carefully read ingredient product labels as well as consult a nutritionist or your physician to determine if a particular recipe meets your dietary needs.

We encourage you to use caution when working with all kitchen equipment and to always follow food safety guidelines.

To purchase this book for business or promotional use or to purchase more than 50 copies at a discount, or for custom editions, please contact Cogin, Inc. at the address below or info@mrfood.com.

Inquiries should be addressed to:
Cogin, Inc.
1770 NW 64 Street, Suite 500
Fort Lauderdale, FL 33309

ISBN: 978-0-9981635-6-7
Printed in the United States of America
Second Edition
www.MrFood.com

Introduction

At the Mr. Food Test Kitchen, we believe in giving home cooks (like you!) the recipes they want. For almost 40 years, we've created recipes that follow the trends you love while sticking to our philosophy of "quick & easy" cooking. So when you asked us to help you make the most of your air fryer, we headed into the Test Kitchen and went to work!

We know that many of you (and yes, even some of our own team members!) may have thought that air-frying was a fad, but the more we worked with them, the more we became convinced that someday air fryers would become a staple in homes across the country. Air-frying not only appeals to health-conscious foodies who crave lightened-up versions of their favorite comfort foods, but to anyone who wants to create great-tasting recipes in less time and with easy clean-up.

The Ultimate Air Fryer Cookbook follows the same quick & easy philosophy as all of our other Mr. Food Test Kitchen cookbooks. Inside, you'll find more than 130 air fryer recipes made with off-the-shelf ingredients that you can find in your local market. And yes, every recipe fits on just one page and has a full-page photo (we know you love it!). Since we know many of you are pressed for time, in this cookbook, we've included specific cooking times for each recipe. (We don't want anyone missing out on In the Kitchen with David!) There are also plenty of helpful tips and tricks to make sure you always end up with tasty results.

Whether you're new to air-frying or have a bit more experience, we're confident that this will become your new go-to cookbook for all things air-frying. With a variety of recipes—everything from rise-and-shine breakfasts to decadent desserts—there's something for everyone. Plus, we tested all of our recipes in various brands and sizes of air fryers to ensure goof-proof results at home. And if you're reading this and still don't have an air fryer, having a book from a trusted friend in the kitchen should give you the confidence to hop on the air fryer train.

Most importantly, we hope you have as much fun using this book as we did creating it for you. So now it's time to roll up your sleeves and start enjoying all that the air fryer can do for you—what you'll end up with is lots of ...

Acknowledgements

Who would think that it would take so many people to create a cookbook? We sure wouldn't have, if we hadn't worked on it ourselves. But the reality is that it does, and we are so thankful that we've assembled such a talented team over the years.

Patty Rosenthal
Test Kitchen Supervisor

Howard Rosenthal
Chief Food Officer

Jodi Flayman
Director of Publishing

Carol Ginsburg
Editor

Merly Mesa
Editor

Victoria Krog
Photographer & Stylist

Lynda Cannon
Test Kitchen Assistant

Dave DiCarlo
Test Kitchen Assistant

Kelly Rusin
Test Kitchen Assistant

Steve Ginsburg
Chief Executive Officer

Hal Silverman
Pre-Press Production
Hal Silverman Studio

Lorraine Dan
Book Design
Grand Design

Table of Contents

Don't Let the Name Fool Ya!

Like many of you, before we had the chance to "get to know" our air fryer, we weren't quite sure what it could do. Was it just a glorified way to cook french fries – one that could make them fast without having to submerge them in a vat of hot oil? The short and the long answer is NO. After testing, tasting, and retesting hundreds of recipes (in an assortment of air fryers), we soon discovered there's a lot more to an air fryer than meets the eye.

With your air fryer you can:

- **Air-fry:** This one is pretty obvious, but for those of you who don't know – you can spritz and toss some of your favorite foods (everything from french fries to Monte Cristos!) with a bit of oil to get that crispy-fried taste you love.

- **Bake:** Your air fryer is basically a compact convection oven which preheats in practically no time. It's perfect for baking small batches, which makes it super energy efficient.

- **Roast:** From prime rib and steak to veggies and pork, your air fryer is the ultimate roasting machine. The hot air circulating inside the air fryer helps seal in the meat's natural juices and brings out the natural goodness in our veggies.

- **Poach/Steam:** All it takes is a little water! After adding it to the air fryer pan, it's up to you to decide what's going in the basket. Maybe you're craving some steamed veggies or a moist and flavorful fish fillet?

- **Toast:** You bet your buns you can use your air fryer to toast anything from an English muffin to a chocolate stuffed croissant! You can even "grill" your grilled cheese. The hot air flow circulating from the top of your air fryer helps to evenly brown bread and other foods. (Just make sure you turn and flip as needed.)

- **Broil:** Since your air fryer cooks with top-down heat, it also acts as the ultimate broiler. Think of it as a way to melt cheese on a burger, make the best onion soup, and on and on.

The Benefits are Many

Now that you know what your air fryer is capable of, what are some of the benefits?

Typically, air fryers are:

- **Fast:** Cooking in an air fryer helps reduce time spent in the kitchen. Not only does it take just about 2 minutes to preheat an air fryer, but we found that recipes cooked between 25 to 30% faster than traditional cooking methods.

- **Safe:** While all kitchen appliances are designed with your safety in mind (that's why it's important to follow the manufacturer's instructions!), we feel that air fryers are easy to use and pretty safe if you follow a few basic rules. Most models feature an easy-to-grab handle, compact design, and built-in safety features.

- **Energy Efficient:** You don't have to have a degree in finance to figure out that an air fryer is friendly on your wallet. Compared to a standard kitchen oven, it draws less than 50% power. With all the money you'll save, your air fryer will practically pay for itself!

- **Compact:** The last thing you need on your counter is a big, bulky appliance that you'll rarely use. Luckily, that's not the case with an air fryer. First of all, they're built to have a small footprint (usually about one square foot), and unlike other kitchen appliances, this one is so easy to work with and clean, you'll find yourself using it several times a week.

- **Healthy:** Everyone wants to eat better, but many of us aren't willing to give up the tastes and textures we love. With an air fryer, you don't have to! A spritz of oil has a lot less fat and calories than submerging your favorite foods in a vat of hot oil or sautéing in gobs of butter. And the basket design allows the fat to drip away!

- **Easy to Clean:** There's no need to scrub, since you can pop the basket and the pan right into your dishwasher. If you prefer to wash these by hand, you be pleasantly surprised at how they practically wipe clean.

Converting Recipes

Did you know you can convert some of your favorite non-air fryer recipes to work in an air fryer? Although the name of this appliance makes it sound more like a fat-free deep fryer, it's not. Now, don't get us wrong, we love how our air fryers "fry", but in order to best understand how to convert recipes that you would normally cook otherwise, you'll need to understand that your air fryer is basically an egg-shaped, countertop convection oven.

To convert recipes, you'll need to start by reducing the temperature by about 25 to 40%. The cooking time is usually reduced 20 to 30%. For example, if you normally cook a roast at 400 degrees for 60 minutes, you would lower the air fryer temperature to 300 degrees and cook it for about 45 minutes. (This is only a rough guide and will vary based on the size and wattage of your air fryer.)

Read the Instruction Manual

With so many varieties of air fryers out there, we strongly urge you to read the instruction manual that comes with yours. It'll help you understand your air fryer and what it can and can't do. Once you have the basics down, you'll feel more confident about using it. Our belief with any kitchen appliance is that you should always respect it, but never fear it.

Test Kitchen Tips

Lucky for you, we've done all the hard work of testing and retesting, which means we've picked up a good set of tips and tricks along the way. Here are some of our favorites (and remember, these are general tips — if a recipe says to do otherwise, always follow the recipe as written):

- **Preheat:** Just like you preheat your oven or heat up a skillet before cooking in it, you also have to preheat your air fryer. However, preheating an air fryer only takes a couple of minutes, which is a real timesaver. Many brands and models have preheat buttons, so it's as easy as touching one button.

- **Find a Pan that Fits:** Some recipes in the book recommend that you cook your food in a pan that is set within the air fryer basket. Since most air fryers will not accommodate a full-sized baking pan, you will need a pan that fits in your air fryer's basket. Many air fryers come with pans, but if yours didn't or isn't the right size, you can always go to wherever they sell kitchen supplies and pick up one up. Usually a 6-inch to 7-inch pan will fit. These come deeper, like the one you see on page 190 filled with our mac and cheese, or shallower, which is what we baked our Chocolate Chunk Jumbo Cookies in on page 282. You can also use any oven-safe pan in your air fryer. Often a 1- to 1-1/2-quart pan will fit in most air fryers. Make sure you check that it fits before you fill it. You can also line the bottom of your air fryer basket with foil to create a customized-sized pan. This is handy when you're in a pinch and don't have the right size pan.

- **Use Foil as a Sling or Makeshift Pan:** Placing food in or removing it from a hot air fryer basket can sometimes be a challenge. That's when a foil sling comes in handy. A foil sling isn't something you buy, it's something you make. First, you start by taking a 12-inch wide piece of aluminum foil and folding it until it's about 4-inches wide. Then you place your pan, or in some cases the food (like a meatloaf) on it and lower it into the pan. Once it's lowered, don't remove it, rather tuck the "straps" (the part that comes up the sides that you hold onto) of the sling neatly inside the basket to prevent them from flapping in the breeze or getting caught in the rotating fan blades.

- **Don't Overcrowd:** This in one tip we urge you never to forget when using your air fryer. Air fryers work by circulating hot air around the food in the basket. An overcrowded basket means restricted air flow, which will result in food that isn't cooked evenly or doesn't crisp up like you want it.

More Test Kitchen Tips

- **Work in Batches:** This tip goes hand-in-hand with not overcrowding your air fryer. Since air fryers come in various sizes, you may need to cook your food in several batches (if it doesn't comfortably fit in the basket).

- **Turn Over:** The heat from an air fryer comes from the top and with the help of a powerful fan, is blown down onto whatever you're cooking. To ensure that all sides are cooked and browned evenly, you'll need to turn the foods over as directed; if not, the top of your food may burn.

- **Prevent Smoking:** One of the benefits of cooking in an air fryer is that it allows the fat to drip through the basket and into the pan below. Since the pan is hot, the drippings may start to smoke. To prevent smoking, when cooking fatty items like meatloaf or bacon, we suggest adding a couple of tablespoons of water to the pan.

- **Add Water to the Pan for Moisture:** Adding some water, broth, or juice to the pan that sits below the basket can also help with keeping foods super moist and flavorful. However, we don't recommend you do this when you're trying to roast veggies or crisp up your fries, as it will actually make them soggy.

- **Spray, Spritz, or Toss:** A little bit of oil on items that you want to "fry" is very important. The key is to add just enough to lightly coat the food. Usually a teaspoon to a tablespoon of oil goes a long way. We like using a spray bottle (that's designed for oil) as a simple way to distribute it easily. You can also use aerosol cooking sprays, if that's what you have on hand.

- **Don't Let Your Food Blow Apart:** Air fryers blow hot air inside the cooking chamber. So to keep the bread of a sandwich in place or your paper-thin slice of cheese on your burger, you may want to secure it with a toothpick. (Just make sure you remove the toothpick before serving.) Also, when breading something like pork chops or chicken, make sure you firmly press the coating on so that it doesn't blow off while cooking.

- **Save the Drippings:** Before you get rid of all the drippings in the pan after roasting meat or poultry, remember that those drippings can be used to add flavor to a sauce. For example, take your steak drippings and add a splash of beef broth or wine for a flavorful steak sauce that takes only seconds.

More Test Kitchen Tips

- **More Than Just for Recipes:** Although this book has more than 130 easy recipes, please don't forget that you can use your air fryer to help prep ingredients too. It makes the best bacon (page 164) and when it comes to croutons, there is no better way to crisp them up. (Page 82). But beyond that, let's not forget you can toast nuts in it (as long as the pieces are not too small and can't fall through the holes in the basket). So experiment and enjoy all that the air fryer has to offer.

- **It's Okay to Peek:** Unlike with an oven, there's no way to see inside your air fryer while it's cooking. And unlike a traditional oven that loses lots of heat every time you open it up, then takes a while to come back to the proper temperature, you can open your air fryer as often as you'd like to check on your food without any major consequences.

- **Keep Things Hot:** Since, at times, you may need to cook a recipe in batches, we suggest that after you cook the first batch, you set it aside while cooking the second one. Right before serving, if the first batch needs to be warmed up, you can place it back into the air fryer along with the second batch for a minute or so to heat it up. Once the coating is set, or the fries, for example, are browned, piling the batches on top of each other is not a problem.

- **The Basket Comes Out First:** Once your food is cooked and you're ready to dump it out onto a platter, don't forget to remove the basket from the pan, first. If you don't, your pan drippings (or that water you placed in the pan to prevent it from smoking or to flavor it) will end up all over your perfectly cooked dish. Plus, the hot liquid or drippings could burn you if you're not careful.

- **Wash after Use:** Although it's easy to place the pan and basket back in the air fryer after cooking and just forget about it, remember that it needs to be washed after each use. So whether you pop the basket and pan in the dishwasher or wash it in the sink (it takes seconds!), a clean air fryer is a happy air fryer.

- **Reheat Leftovers:** Your microwave might become a bit jealous of your new-found appliance when it comes to heating leftovers. Just wait till you discover how good a slice of pizza tastes when it's been reheated in an air fryer rather than a microwave. When heating up leftovers in an air fryer, keep the temperature on the lower side so that the center of the food gets hot without burning the outside. You can also wrap food in foil to cook it more evenly inside and out.

Welcome to the Mr. Food Test Kitchen Family!

Whether you've been a fan of the Mr. Food Test Kitchen for years or were just recently introduced to us, we want to welcome you into our kitchen...and our family. Even though we've grown in many ways over the years, the one thing that hasn't changed is our philosophy for quick & easy cooking.

Over 40 years ago we began by sharing our recipes with you through the television screen. Today, not only is the Mr. Food Test Kitchen TV segment syndicated all over the country, but we've also proudly published over 50 best-selling cookbooks. That's not to mention our hugely popular websites, MrFood.com and EverydayDiabeticRecipes.com. And for those of you who love to get social, we do too! You can find us online on Facebook, Twitter, Pinterest, and Instagram—boy, do we love connecting with you!

If you've got a passion for cooking (like we do!), then you know that the only thing better than curling up with a cookbook and drooling over the pictures is actually getting to taste the finished recipes. That's why we give you simple step-by-step instructions that make it feel like we're in your kitchen guiding you along the way. Your taste buds will be celebrating in no time!

So whether you're new to the family or you've been a part of it from the beginning, we want to thank you. You can bet there is always room at our table for you, because there's nothing better than sharing in all of the... "OOH IT'S SO GOOD!!®"

Patty   Howard   Kelly

Other titles you may enjoy from the Mr. Food Test Kitchen:

Christmas Made Easy

Quick & Easy Comfort Cookbook

Sinful Sweets & Tasty Treats

Just One More Bite!

Hello Taste, Goodbye Guilt! (Diabetic Friendly)

Guilt-Free Weeknight Favorites (Diabetic Friendly)

Guilt-Free Comfort Favorites (Diabetic Friendly)

Cook it Slow, Cook it Fast

Wheel of Fortune Collectible Cookbook

The Ultimate Cooking for Two Cookbook

The Ultimate Cake Mix & More Cookbook

The Ultimate 30 Minutes or Less Cookbook

The Ultimate Recipes Across America Cookbook

As always, we remember our founder, Art Ginsburg, who believed that everyone would cook if only we could make it quick & easy (and thanks to air fryers we can). We thank you for allowing us to carry on this tradition.

Eye-Opening Breakfasts

Ham & Cheese Breakfast Bundles

This just might be the most perfect breakfast for someone on-the-go. You can make a batch on the weekend and simply reheat them throughout the week for a quick morning meal. They're filled with lots of cheesy, egg and ham goodness, so you can feel full and satisfied too. If a good breakfast is truly the most important meal of the day, then this is a page you'll want to dog-ear!

Makes 8

Ingredients

1 tablespoon butter

3 eggs, divided

1 tablespoon plus 1 teaspoon water, divided

¼ cup diced ham

1 (16.3-ounce) package refrigerated biscuits (8 biscuits)

⅓ cup shredded cheddar cheese

EVERYTHING TOPPING

½ teaspoon sesame seeds

½ teaspoon caraway seeds

½ teaspoon onion powder

¼ teaspoon kosher salt

¼ teaspoon poppy seeds

So Many Options: To change these up, feel free to experiment with different kinds of shredded cheese or topping blends.

Preparation

1 In a small skillet over medium heat, melt butter. In a small bowl, whisk 2 eggs with 1 tablespoon water; mix well. Pour eggs into skillet, add ham, and scramble until light and fluffy.

2 Separate biscuits and place on a cutting board. With your fingers, flatten each biscuit, so each one is about 4-inches round. Evenly spoon egg mixture onto center of each biscuit and top eggs with cheese. Gather edges of each biscuit around filling and pinch to secure. Place seam-side down on cutting board.

3 Preheat air fryer to 320 degrees F. Meanwhile, in a small bowl, combine all ingredients for the Everything Topping; mix well. In another small bowl, whisk remaining egg with remaining 1 teaspoon of water and brush top of each biscuit bundle with egg mixture, then sprinkle with Everything Topping.

4 Coat air fryer basket with cooking spray. Working in batches, if necessary, place bundles in basket without overcrowding. Air-fry 8 to 9 minutes or until dough is cooked through and crust is golden. Remove from basket and repeat if necessary.

Supreme Breakfast Pit-zza

Who's going to turn down a freshly made breakfast pizza? Not anyone we know! When pizza is cooked in an air fryer, the hot air circulating around the pizza gives it a crispy, golden crust without drying out the toppings. And since it cooks in just minutes, it's both weekday and weekend friendly. In fact, we're sensing a lot of breakfast pizzas in your future.

Makes 2

Ingredients

2 (6-inch) pita breads

Cooking spray

3 eggs

1 tablespoon water

¼ teaspoon salt

⅛ teaspoon black pepper

1 tablespoon vegetable oil

¼ cup chopped onion

¼ cup chopped green bell pepper

½ cup sliced mushrooms

½ cup shredded mozzarella cheese, divided

8 slices pepperoni

Preparation

1 Preheat air fryer to 360 degrees F. Coat top of one pita with cooking spray and place in air fryer basket; air-fry 2 minutes. Turn it over and continue to cook 2 more minutes or until golden. Remove from basket and repeat with second pita.

2 Meanwhile, in a medium bowl, whisk eggs, water, salt, and black pepper; set aside. In a medium skillet over medium heat, heat vegetable oil until hot. Sauté onion, bell pepper, and mushrooms 2 to 3 minutes or until tender; set aside. In the same skillet, scramble eggs until fluffy.

3 Sprinkle half the cheese evenly over warmed pitas and top each with half the scrambled eggs. Evenly divide vegetable mixture and pepperoni over eggs.

4 Using a sling (see page ix), place one pita pizza in basket and cook 2 minutes or until cheese is melted. Repeat with second pita pizza. Cut into wedges and enjoy.

Bacon-Wrapped Potato Tot Skewers

We love diners where the home fries are served right off the griddle, and you can practically taste the bacon that cooked right alongside them. In our version of this classic diner combo, you get perfectly cooked bacon (thank you, air fryer!) wrapped around golden and delicious potato tots. What a tasty way to start any day!

Makes 8 skewers

Ingredients

12 slices bacon

Coarsely ground black pepper for sprinkling

24 frozen potato tots (about 7 ounces)

8 (4-inch) bamboo skewers, soaked in water for 5-10 minutes

Preparation

1 Preheat air fryer to 370 degrees F.

2 Lay bacon out on a cutting board and sprinkle with pepper. Cut each strip in half crosswise. Wrap each potato tot with a half strip of bacon. Skewer 3 bacon-wrapped potato tots onto each bamboo skewer, leaving about ½-inch between each, as shown in the photo.

3 Coat air fryer basket with cooking spray; place half of the skewers in it. Air-fry 6 minutes, then turn over and cook 3 to 4 more minutes or until bacon is cooked to desired doneness.

4 Remove first batch from basket and repeat with remaining skewers. Serve immediately or cover and set aside. When the second batch is done, you can reheat the first batch by placing them in the basket 1 minute or until hot.

Maple-Glazed Breakfast Sausage

Have you ever "accidentally" poured maple syrup on your sausage or bacon while you were aiming for your stack of pancakes? Admit it, of course you have. Don't worry, we can understand why! It's because the sweet syrup is the perfect complement to the savory sausage. And although we're big fans of store-bought breakfast sausage, we think our homemade version is pretty remarkable. How about you give it a try and let us know what you think?

Makes 16

Ingredients

1 pound ground pork

¾ teaspoon salt

¾ teaspoon black pepper

2 teaspoons ground sage

⅛ teaspoon ground nutmeg

2 tablespoons maple syrup

Preparation

1 Preheat air fryer to 400 degrees F.

2 In a medium bowl, combine all ingredients except maple syrup; mix well. Form mixture into 16 equal patties.

3 Coat air fryer basket with cooking spray. Working in batches, place patties in basket, being careful not to overcrowd. Air-fry 5 minutes; turn over. Brush tops with maple syrup and continue to cook 2 to 3 more minutes or until no longer pink in center. Repeat with remaining patties. When the last batch is done, you can reheat the previous batches by placing them in the basket 1 minute or until hot. Serve immediately.

Test Kitchen Tip: Only need a few patties? No problem! These freeze great before they're cooked, so freeze whatever you don't need right now and cook them when you need them. (If you cook them from frozen add a couple of minutes to the cooking time.)

Strawberry Cheesecake French Toast

We hope you're as blown away by the crispiness of this overstuffed French toast as we were the first time we tested this recipe! Since then, we've made it over and over again with amazing results every time. The famous quote, "An army marches on its stomach," implies that we all work best when our bellies are full. Here in the Test Kitchen, we wholeheartedly agree!

Serves 2

Ingredients

½ (8-ounce) package cream cheese, softened

2 tablespoons confectioners' sugar, plus extra for sprinkling

2 tablespoons strawberry preserves

4 (1-inch-thick) slices challah bread

2 eggs

¼ cup milk

1 teaspoon vanilla extract

2 cups coarsely crushed sweetened cornflake cereal

Preparation

1 In a small bowl, combine cream cheese and 2 tablespoons confectioners' sugar; mix well, then stir in preserves. Spread evenly over 2 slices of bread. Top with remaining bread, forming 2 sandwiches.

2 In a shallow bowl, whisk eggs, milk, and vanilla until well combined. In another shallow bowl, place the crushed cereal.

3 Dip one sandwich into egg mixture, coating both sides, then into cereal, firmly pressing coating onto both sides. Preheat air fryer to 370 degrees F. Coat air fryer basket with cooking spray. Place sandwich in basket. Air-fry 4 minutes, turn over, and continue to cook 2 to 3 more minutes or until golden brown.

4 Remove from basket and repeat with remaining sandwich. Cover and set aside. When the second sandwich is done, you can reheat the first one by placing it in the basket 1 minute or until hot. Sprinkle with confectioners' sugar and enjoy.

10-Minute Sausage Pancake Muffins

If you've got 10 minutes, then we want to introduce you to a breakfast that we know you're gonna love. Although these took several tries for us to perfect, they're pretty much goof proof now. These sausage-stuffed, pancake-like muffins are perfectly moist and delicious from the inside out. All you need is a little maple syrup and breakfast is ready.

Makes 8

Ingredients

1 cup pancake and baking mix

1 tablespoon sugar

1 egg

½ cup milk

¼ cup club soda

2 teaspoons vegetable oil

3 frozen breakfast sausage links, cut into ¼-inch pieces

Pancake syrup for drizzling

Preparation

1 Preheat air fryer to 350 degrees F. Coat 8 foil muffin cup liners with cooking spray and set aside. (You can pick up the foil muffin cup liners in the baking aisle at your supermarket. Paper liners will not work here.)

2 In a large bowl, combine pancake and baking mix, sugar, egg, milk, club soda, and oil; mix well. Stir in sausage pieces.

3 Place 4 muffin cup liners in air fryer basket. (Yes you put these in empty – it's much easier to fill them that way.) Fill each muffin cup liner about ⅔ full. Air-fry 8 to 10 minutes or until a toothpick inserted in center comes out clean and tops are golden. Remove from air fryer and repeat with remaining batter. When the second batch is done, you can reheat the first batch by placing them in the basket 1 minute or until hot. Serve warm, drizzled with pancake syrup.

Hash Brown "Waffles"

No waffle maker needed here, just a bunch of creativity and a passion for thinking outside the box. By using a shallow 6-inch pan, you can make perfectly-sized, homemade potato "waffles" in your air fryer. Even though these are in the breakfast chapter, and are great served with eggs, we think they're just as fitting for dinner (especially when they're teamed up with our Truly Southern "Fried" Chicken, page 108).

Makes 3

Ingredients

1 [20-ounce] package refrigerated shredded hash browns

2 eggs, beaten

2 tablespoons all-purpose flour

¼ cup chopped scallion

½ teaspoon garlic powder

¼ teaspoon paprika

½ teaspoon salt

¼ teaspoon black pepper

Cooking spray

Preparation

1 Preheat air fryer to 400 degrees F. Coat a shallow 6-inch pan with cooking spray. (Many air fryers come with a pan like this, but if yours didn't, you can use any 6-inch, oven-safe pan or you can pick one up wherever kitchen products are sold.)

2 In a large bowl, combine hash browns, eggs, flour, scallion, garlic powder, paprika, salt, and pepper; mix well. Pour 1 cup of hash brown mixture into pan, gently pressing mixture down with your fingers. Place pan in air fryer basket.

3 Air-fry 10 minutes. Carefully remove pan and invert waffle onto a plate. Place waffle back into pan, bottom-side up, and continue to cook 7 to 8 more minutes or until golden. Cover to keep warm. Repeat with remaining hash brown mixture. When the third waffle is done, you can reheat the others by placing them in basket 1 minute or until hot.

Apple Cinnamon Danish

Shh! We're going to let you in on a little secret. This recipe started out as a disaster! At first, we were trying to make a pull-apart apple bread. Unfortunately, the results were a gooey mess. Rather than giving up (we're sure glad we didn't!), we discovered that if we "bake" these more like danish, they are absolutely perfect. Plus, this way you get lots more of the yummy glaze with every bite.

Makes 16

Ingredients

3 tablespoons butter, melted

1 teaspoon vanilla extract

3 tablespoons brown sugar

1 tablespoon granulated sugar

1 teaspoon ground cinnamon

1 small apple, peeled, cored, and finely diced

1 (16.3-ounce) package refrigerated buttermilk biscuits (8 biscuits)

3 tablespoons milk

1 cup confectioners' sugar

Preparation

1 In a small bowl, mix together butter and vanilla. In another small bowl, combine brown sugar, granulated sugar, and cinnamon; mix well. Reserve 2 tablespoons for later. Stir apples into cinnamon-sugar mixture.

2 Separate biscuits and place on a cutting board. Using your fingers, separate each biscuit into 2 layers, making a total of 16 biscuit rounds. Brush each biscuit with butter mixture, and top with a heaping tablespoon of apple mixture. Sprinkle each biscuit evenly with reserved cinnamon-sugar mixture. Preheat air fryer to 350 degrees F.

3 Coat air fryer basket with cooking spray. Working in batches, place biscuits in basket without overcrowding, and air-fry 7 to 8 minutes or until golden and danish are cooked through. Remove from basket and repeat with remaining biscuits.

4 Meanwhile, in a small bowl, combine milk and confectioners' sugar, and whisk until smooth. Drizzle over danish and serve.

Homemade Bakery Donuts

If you've never made donuts at home before, then you're in for a real treat. What makes these so good is that there's no greasy mess to deal with and they're super easy. Plus, since we start with a supermarket shortcut, there's no kneading or proofing required. That means all you have to worry about is what fun toppings you're gonna dress 'em up with. What are your favorites?

Makes 8

Ingredients

1 (16.3-ounce) package refrigerated biscuits (8 biscuits)

Cooking spray

Assorted toppings (see below for some of our favorite combinations)

S'mores Donuts: *Frost with chocolate frosting, then top with crushed graham crackers, mini marshmallows, and chocolate chips.*

Rainbow Donuts: *Frost with vanilla frosting, and finish them off with your favorite, colorful breakfast cereal.*

Peanut Butter Cup Donuts: *Frost with chocolate frosting and top with cut-up, mini peanut butter cups (and crumbled bacon if you're feeling really adventurous!).*

Lemon Cream Donuts: *Frost with vanilla frosting, then drizzle with lemon curd. The combo is amazing!*

Preparation

1 Preheat air fryer to 320 degrees F. Separate biscuits and lay them flat on a cutting board. Using an apple corer or bottle cap, cut out a small circle in center of each biscuit, creating a donut shape. Set donut holes aside.

2 Coat bottom of air fryer basket with cooking spray. Working in batches, spray both sides of dough with cooking spray and place in basket, leaving space between each one so they can expand while cooking.

3 Air-fry 4 minutes; turn over, and continue to cook 3 more minutes or until golden. Remove to a wire rack to cool and repeat with remaining dough. (Rather than discarding the donut holes, air-fry them! They take about 3 minutes. Just make sure to coat them with cooking spray before cooking and shake the basket a couple of times halfway through cooking time, so they cook evenly.)

4 Frost and decorate as desired.

Rise & Shine Banana Muffins

The first time we were introduced to the air fryer, we thought the only thing we'd be able to cook in it would be french fries and frozen chicken nuggets. Boy, were we wrong! Once we discovered you could also "bake" in it, the possibilities were endless. Just take a look at these fresh muffins we made, without ever turning on the oven! You're gonna love 'em.

Makes 6

Ingredients

½ stick butter, softened

½ cup plus 1 tablespoon sugar, divided

1 egg

1 ripe banana, mashed

¾ cup chopped walnuts, divided

¾ cup all-purpose flour

½ teaspoon baking soda

Preparation

1 Coat 6 parchment paper or foil muffin cup liners with cooking spray.

2 In a large bowl, beat butter and ½ cup sugar until creamy. Add egg and beat until light and fluffy. Stir in banana and ½ cup walnuts. Add flour and baking soda, mixing just until moistened.

3 In a small bowl, combine remaining ¼ cup walnuts and remaining 1 tablespoon sugar; mix well.

4 Spoon batter evenly into muffin liners; sprinkle with nut mixture. Preheat air fryer to 350 degrees F. Place 3 filled liners in air fryer basket and air-fry 15 to 17 minutes, or until a toothpick inserted in center comes out clean; let cool. Repeat with remaining 3 muffins.

Amazing Appetizers

Mini Mexican Egg Rolls

Welcome to our version of fusion cooking. In case you're not familiar with fusion cooking, it's when you blend a few ethnic or regional styles of cooking into a single dish. We did just that by filling crispy, Asian-style wonton skins with a south-of-the-border filling that'll knock your socks off. And thanks to the air fryer, we can keep these on the healthier side by "frying" them with only a spritz of oil.

Makes 24

Ingredients

½ cup black beans, rinsed and drained

½ cup frozen corn, thawed

½ cup shredded Monterey Jack cheese

½ cup salsa

1 teaspoon ground cumin

1 cup shredded cooked chicken

1 tablespoon chopped fresh cilantro

24 wonton wrappers

Cooking spray

AVOCADO DIPPING SAUCE

1 avocado, pitted and cut into chunks

½ cup sour cream

1 tablespoon chopped fresh cilantro

1 tablespoon lime juice

¼ teaspoon salt

Preparation

1. In a medium bowl, combine black beans, corn, cheese, salsa, and cumin; mix well. Stir in chicken and 1 tablespoon cilantro.

2. Place 6 wonton wrappers on a cutting board with 1 corner pointing toward you. Spoon 1 heaping teaspoon of chicken mixture onto center of each wrapper. Lightly brush edges with water. Fold the corner nearest you over the mixture, then fold and tuck in both sides, envelope-style; roll up tightly. Place seam-side down on a platter. Repeat with remaining wontons and filling. Coat lightly with cooking spray.

3. Preheat air fryer to 400 degrees F.

4. Coat air fryer basket with cooking spray. Place half the egg rolls in basket. Air-fry 3 to 4 minutes or until golden; turn over, spray lightly, and continue to cook 3 to 4 more minutes or until golden. Repeat with remaining egg rolls. When the second batch is done, throw the first batch back in for 1 minute to warm up.

5. Meanwhile, to make Avocado Dipping Sauce, in a food processor or blender, combine all sauce ingredients; blend until smooth. Serve egg rolls immediately with dipping sauce.

Magical Dilly Potato Puffs

When it came to naming these, the Test Kitchen team was divided. One half wanted to call these Silly Dilly Potato Puffs, since they're packed with fresh dill. The other half was in favor of Magical Potato Puffs since the crust magically develops as they cook. We ended up coming to a compromise, but we'd love to know what you'd have named them. Go ahead and let us know on social media!

Makes 24

Ingredients

1 pound russet potatoes, peeled and cut into chunks

1 tablespoon vegetable oil

½ cup chopped onion

⅓ cup bread crumbs

1 teaspoon chopped fresh dill

¾ teaspoon salt

⅛ teaspoon black pepper

1 egg yolk, beaten

Serving Suggestion: *If you're going to dip 'em, we suggest going with a spicy mustard or a creamy dill dressing. The flavors pair perfectly!*

Preparation

1 Place potatoes in a large saucepan and add just enough water to cover them. Bring to a boil over high heat, then reduce heat to medium and cook 12 to 15 minutes or until fork-tender; drain well. Place in a large bowl.

2 Meanwhile, in a small skillet over medium heat, heat oil until hot. Sauté onion 3 to 4 minutes or until tender. Add sautéed onion, bread crumbs, dill, salt, and pepper to hot potatoes. With a potato masher or electric mixer, mash until smooth and well combined. Allow to cool slightly.

3 Preheat air fryer to 380 degrees F.

4 Coat air fryer basket with cooking spray. When potato mixture is cooled just enough to handle, roll into 24 (1-inch) balls, using your hands, and place on a work surface. Lightly brush with egg yolk, covering completely, and place as many as will fit in the basket without overcrowding.

5 Air-fry 8 to 9 minutes or until golden. Carefully remove from basket and repeat with remaining potato balls, if necessary. When second batch is done, toss the first batch back in to warm up.

Shortcut Spanakopita Bites

We love spanakopita here in the Test Kitchen; however, we'll admit that working with the dough can be kind of challenging. So, rather than stressing out, we've come up with a shortcut version. These deliver the same taste and crunch you love, without a whole lot of work. By the way, we suggest serving them on paper plates since, as you know, Greek parties can get kind of wild. Opa!

Makes 30

Ingredients

½ (8-ounce) package cream cheese, softened

2 tablespoons mayonnaise

1 teaspoon lemon juice

½ teaspoon oregano

½ teaspoon garlic powder

¼ teaspoon salt

1 cup frozen chopped spinach, thawed and squeezed dry

¼ cup feta cheese crumbles

2 (1.9-ounce) packages frozen mini phyllo shells (30 shells total)

6 pitted Kalamata olives, thinly sliced

Preparation

1 In a medium bowl, combine cream cheese, mayonnaise, lemon juice, oregano, garlic powder, and salt; mix well. Stir in spinach and feta cheese just until combined; do not overmix. Spoon about 1 tablespoon of mixture into each phyllo shell.

2 Preheat air fryer to 380 degrees F.

3 Coat air fryer basket with cooking spray. Place half the phyllo shells in basket. Air-fry 3 to 4 minutes or until crispy and heated through. Repeat with remaining shells or see Tip. Top with olive slices and serve.

Test Kitchen Tip: *If you don't need to make all of these at once, you can freeze the rest before cooking. Simply freeze these in the trays that the phyllo cups come in and when you want to serve them, pop them in the air fryer, frozen. You may need to add a minute or so to the time suggested above.*

Secret Ingredient Cocktail Meatballs

We've all been there – you take a bite of something that's really good, and sit there puzzling over what makes it taste that way. Is it the spices? Maybe it's the way it's cooked? Could it be kitchen magic? Often times, it's just one special, secret ingredient. And that's just the case here. Make these for your friends and family, and see if they can figure it out. You can even give 'em a hint: it's "doctor" approved!

Makes 24

Ingredients

1 pound ground beef

⅓ cup seasoned bread crumbs

1 egg

4 tablespoons water, divided

2 tablespoons finely chopped onion

½ teaspoon salt, divided

½ teaspoon black pepper, divided

1 cup ketchup

1 cup cherry cola
(we used Dr. Pepper®)

¼ cup hoisin sauce

1 clove garlic, minced

Preparation

1 Add 2 tablespoons of water to bottom of air fryer pan. (This will prevent the drippings from smoking while cooking.)

2 In a large bowl, combine ground beef, bread crumbs, egg, remaining 2 tablespoons water, the onion, ¼ teaspoon salt, and ¼ teaspoon black pepper; mix well. Form into 24 (1-inch) meatballs. Preheat air fryer to 380 degrees F.

3 Coat air fryer basket with cooking spray. Place half the meatballs in basket and air-fry 5 to 6 minutes or until meatballs are cooked through, removing the basket and gently shaking halfway through cooking. (This way they'll cook evenly.) Remove from basket and repeat with remaining meatballs.

4 Meanwhile, in a large skillet over medium heat, combine ketchup, cola, hoisin sauce, garlic, remaining ¼ teaspoon salt, and ¼ teaspoon pepper, and bring just to a boil. Reduce heat to low, add meatballs from both batches, and cook 3 to 5 minutes or until heated through, stirring occasionally.

Fried Green Tomatoes with Cheesy Grits

If you live in the South or have had the good fortune to eat while visiting there, then there's a pretty good chance you've had fried green tomatoes. If you haven't, here's your opportunity to do so. This Southern classic cooks up easily in an air fryer and is made even more perfect when topped with another Southern favorite – cheesy grits! Ya'll are really gonna impress friends and family with this one.

Makes about 15

Ingredients

½ cup all-purpose flour

½ cup self-rising cornmeal mix

1 teaspoon salt

¼ teaspoon black pepper

1 egg

1-¼ cups water, divided

3 green tomatoes, ends trimmed and cut into ½-inch slices

¼ cup grits

⅓ cup shredded cheddar cheese

2 tablespoons chopped fresh chives

Cracked black pepper (optional)

Preparation

1 In a shallow dish, combine flour, cornmeal, salt, and pepper; mix well. In a large bowl, whisk egg and ¼ cup water. Add tomato slices, in batches, and toss to coat. Dip each tomato slice in flour mixture, completely. Preheat air fryer to 400 degrees F.

2 Coat air fryer basket with cooking spray. Place enough tomato slices in basket to line the bottom, making sure they don't overlap, and lightly spray with cooking spray. Air-fry 8 minutes, turn over, and continue to cook 8 to 9 more minutes or until crispy. (The breading will remain very light in color, so no worries if these don't get golden brown.) Remove to a plate and cover to keep warm. Repeat with remaining tomato slices.

3 Meanwhile, in a small saucepan over medium high heat, bring remaining 1 cup water to a boil; add grits, cover, and reduce heat to low. Simmer 15 minutes or until grits are softened. Stir in cheese and continue to simmer until cheese is melted.

4 When ready to serve, place tomatoes on a platter and top each with a dollop of cheesy grits; sprinkle with chives and cracked pepper, if desired.

Cheesy Italian Pepper Poppers

Before you think of skipping this recipe because it sounds like it might be spicy, we have to tell you – there's nothing spicy about these pepper poppers. In fact, the only tears you'll have from eating these are tears of joy. That's because we stuffed mini sweet peppers with a dreamy, creamy filling, sort of like what you might expect to find in stuffed shells. Dish these up with some marinara sauce and get poppin'!

Makes 18

Ingredients

1 (8-ounce) package cream cheese

¾ cup shredded mozzarella cheese

¼ cup chopped fresh basil

1 teaspoon Italian seasoning

1 teaspoon garlic powder

¼ teaspoon salt

9 mini sweet peppers, split in half lengthwise, seeds removed

¼ cup all-purpose flour

½ cup Italian bread crumbs

2 eggs, beaten

1 tablespoon water

Cooking spray

Preparation

1 In a medium bowl, combine cream cheese, mozzarella cheese, basil, Italian seasoning, garlic powder, and salt; mix well. Spoon a heaping teaspoon of cream cheese mixture into each pepper half; set aside.

2 Place flour and bread crumbs in 2 separate shallow bowls. In a small bowl, whisk together eggs and water. Dip stuffed pepper halves into flour, then into egg mixture, and then bread crumbs, coating completely. (Be sure to press bread crumbs firmly onto peppers so they don't blow off in the air fryer.)

3 Preheat air fryer to 380 degrees F.

4 Coat air fryer basket with cooking spray. Working in batches, place peppers cheese-side up in basket, making sure not to overcrowd, and spray lightly with cooking spray. Air-fry 4 to 5 minutes or until heated through and golden. Repeat with remaining peppers. Serve warm.

Green Bean Fries with Citrus Aioli

We've come a long way since the days when the only fries folks would eat were the potato kind. Nowadays, we're frying (or air frying!) all kinds of veggies. One of our favorites is still the green bean. The way we make these, they're perfectly snack-worthy. After all, between the crunchy Parmesan coating and the homemade citrus aioli, it's hard not to love 'em.

Serves 6

Ingredients

1-½ cups panko bread crumbs

½ cup grated Parmesan cheese

1 teaspoon garlic powder

¾ teaspoon salt

2 eggs

¼ cup all-purpose flour

1 pound fresh green beans, trimmed

Cooking spray

CITRUS AIOLI

½ cup mayonnaise

2 tablespoons orange marmalade

2 tablespoons olive oil

⅛ teaspoon salt

Preparation

1 In a shallow dish, combine bread crumbs, Parmesan cheese, garlic powder, and salt; mix well. In another shallow dish, whisk eggs. Put the flour in a third shallow dish.

2 Working with a few at a time, coat each green bean with flour, then egg, and finally, coat completely in bread crumb mixture, pressing firmly onto each bean. Preheat air fryer to 380 degrees F. Coat air fryer basket with cooking spray. Place a single layer of beans in basket, then place another layer of beans in the opposite direction on top of first layer. Lightly spray beans with cooking spray.

3 Air-fry 5 to 6 minutes or until golden brown and crispy, shaking basket halfway through cooking to ensure they brown evenly. Gently remove from basket and repeat with remaining beans.

4 Meanwhile, to make the Citrus Aioli, simply combine aioli ingredients in a mini food processor or blender and process until smooth. Drizzle over beans and enjoy.

Wrapped-Up Cheesy Pickles

If you've never had these, then you might be thinking that this combo of flavors and textures sounds a little bit … weird. You know what? You're right! But just because something is weird, doesn't mean it can't be amazing too. This combo delivers tart goodness, cheesy yumminess, and crispy wowness. All together, it's a winning appetizer worthy of being served any time.

Makes 10

Ingredients

1 (8-ounce) block mozzarella cheese

10 egg roll wrappers

1 (24-ounce) jar dill pickle spears, drained and patted dry

Cooking spray

Serving Suggestion: If you've got a bottle of ranch dressing in your fridge, now's a good time to bring it out. These taste even more amazing when dunked into some ranch!

Preparation

1 Place the cheese on a cutting board and cut into 5 long strips, then cut each strip in half lengthwise so that it's about the size of a pickle spear.

2 Place an egg roll wrapper on a cutting board with a corner pointing toward you. Place a piece of cheese across center, then top with a pickle spear. Lightly brush edges with water. Fold the corner nearest you over the pickle, then fold and tuck in both sides, envelope-style; roll up tightly. Repeat with remaining wrappers, cheese, and pickles. Preheat air fryer to 400 degrees F.

3 Coat air fryer basket with cooking spray. Working in batches, place wrapped pickles in basket, seam-side down, making sure not to overcrowd them. Lightly spray with cooking spray on all sides. Air-fry 4 minutes, turn over, and continue cooking 2 to 3 more minutes or until golden. Repeat with remaining wrapped pickles. When the last batch is done, you can reheat the previous batches in the basket for 1 minute or until hot.

Pepperoni Pizza Stuffed Mushrooms

Did you know that February 4th is National Stuffed Mushroom Day? No, you don't get the day off from work and banks aren't closed. However, you do get to enjoy a day where it's totally okay to eat as many of your favorite stuffed mushrooms as you want. With that in mind, we came up with a twist on traditional stuffed mushrooms you're going to love. These are sure to make you feel like a ... fungi! (Pun intended!)

Makes 12

Ingredients

1 pound large fresh mushrooms

2 tablespoons butter

⅓ cup Italian-style bread crumbs

⅓ cup chopped pepperoni slices

½ teaspoon dried oregano

½ teaspoon garlic powder

¼ teaspoon salt

⅓ cup pizza sauce

¼ cup shredded mozzarella cheese

Preparation

1 Gently clean mushrooms by wiping them with damp paper towels. Remove stems from 12 mushrooms; set aside caps. Finely chop mushroom stems and any remaining whole mushrooms.

2 In a medium skillet over medium heat, melt butter; sauté chopped mushrooms 3 to 4 minutes or until tender. Remove from heat and stir in bread crumbs, pepperoni, oregano, garlic powder, salt, and pizza sauce; mix well.

3 Using a teaspoon (the kind you use with your tea, not to measure with), stuff mushroom caps with stuffing mixture. Preheat air fryer to 350 degrees F.

4 Coat air fryer basket with cooking spray. Place as many of the mushrooms in basket as will fit, making sure not to overcrowd, and air-fry 4 minutes. Sprinkle each with mozzarella cheese and continue to cook 1 more minute or until cheese is melted and mushrooms are heated through. Repeat with remaining mushrooms if necessary. Serve immediately.

Make-Your-Own Potato Skins Bar

These pint-sized potato skins are going to be a hit at your next get-together. To make them, we sort of "bake" them until they're tender. Then after scooping out the pulp, we air-fry them until they're crispy. Whether you serve these at your family reunion or during the holidays, you can bet everyone's going to be talking about 'em.

Makes about 36 halves

Ingredients

1 (28-ounce) bag baby red potatoes (creamers)

1 tablespoon vegetable oil

1 teaspoon kosher salt

Preparation

1 Preheat air fryer to 360 degrees F. Add whole potatoes to air fryer basket, working in batches if necessary, and air-fry 18 to 20 minutes or until fork-tender.

2 Remove potatoes from basket, let cool slightly, then cut each in half. (Careful, these babies are gonna be hot!) Using a spoon, scoop out some of the potato pulp, leaving about ¼-inch of the pulp around the edges. (Save scooped potato pulp for another use.)

3 In a large bowl, toss potato skins with oil and kosher salt, coating evenly. Return potato skins to basket, working in batches if necessary, and cook at 400 degrees F for 8 to 9 minutes or until crispy. Make sure you shake the basket a couple of times during cooking to ensure potatoes brown evenly.

4 Serve potato skins with bowls of everyone's favorite toppings, like sour cream, shredded cheddar cheese, chili, scallions, and crumbled bacon.

Sweet & Sour Chicken Wings

Before the air fryer, if you wanted really crispy wings, you had to deep-fry them. But now things have changed! The air fryer allows us to "fry" these without tacking on any extra calories or fat. More importantly, it delivers results that taste just like they came out of a deep fryer. So, rejoice! With wings that taste this good, you'll be sucking every last bit of the homemade sauce off the bones, without the guilt!

Serves 5

Ingredients

2 pounds split chicken wings, thawed if frozen

2 teaspoons vegetable oil

½ teaspoon salt

¼ cup all-purpose flour

Cooking spray

½ cup sweet and sour sauce

¼ cup honey

¼ cup Thai sweet chili sauce

2 teaspoons soy sauce

2 cloves garlic, chopped

½ teaspoon ground ginger

Preparation

1 Preheat air fryer to 400 degrees F.

2 In a large bowl, toss wings with oil and salt. Add flour and toss until wings are evenly coated. Place wings in air fryer basket, then lightly spray with cooking spray. Air-fry 13 to 15 minutes or until crispy; turn wings over, lightly spray again with cooking spray, and continue to cook 13 to 15 more minutes or until crispy.

3 Meanwhile, in a large bowl, combine sweet and sour sauce, honey, chili sauce, soy sauce, garlic, and ginger; mix well. Add wings to sauce and toss until evenly coated; serve immediately.

Amazing Shrimp Cocktail

Shrimp cocktail is a classic appetizer that dates back to the '60s. As good as it is, we don't often hear anyone rave about how amazing it is. Well, that's all about to change! Our shrimp is seasoned and air-fried, rather than just boiled. And, if that isn't enough, we created an addictive remoulade dipping sauce that puts most cocktail sauces to shame. Are you ready for all the raves?

Serves 6

Ingredients

1 tablespoon olive oil

1 teaspoon seafood seasoning (we used Old Bay®)

½ teaspoon lemon zest

1 pound peeled uncooked colossal shrimp with tails on (14-16)

REMOULADE SAUCE

½ cup mayonnaise

2 tablespoons stone ground mustard

1 tablespoon horseradish

½ teaspoon paprika

¼ teaspoon salt

⅛ teaspoon black pepper

½ teaspoon lemon juice

Preparation

1 Preheat air fryer to 400 degrees F.

2 In a large bowl, combine oil, seafood seasoning, and lemon zest; mix well. Add shrimp and toss until evenly coated.

3 Coat air fryer basket with cooking spray. Place shrimp in basket and air-fry 4 to 5 minutes or until shrimp turn pink and edges begin to get crispy, shaking basket halfway through cooking.

4 Meanwhile, in a small bowl, mix Remoulade Sauce ingredients until thoroughly combined. Serve shrimp with sauce and enjoy.

Show-Stopping Cherry Pecan Brie

It may look like a lot of work, but to tell you the truth, this recipe is absolutely easy. (On the other hand, it might not be a bad idea to tell everyone that it took you all day to create this masterpiece...) The center is ooey-gooey and the cherry pecan sauce is all it takes for this to be the first dish that disappears at any open house.

Serves 8

Ingredients

1 (8-ounce) round Brie cheese

1 teaspoon brown sugar

2 tablespoons butter

½ cup coarsely chopped pecans

¼ cup maple syrup

½ teaspoon orange zest

¼ teaspoon ground cinnamon

¼ cup dried cherries

Preparation

1 Preheat air fryer to 330 degrees F.

2 Coat air fryer basket with cooking spray. Place cheese in basket; sprinkle brown sugar on top of cheese and press down lightly. Air-fry 6 to 8 minutes or until cheese begins to soften.

3 Meanwhile, in a small skillet over low heat, melt butter. Add pecans and toast 3 minutes. Add syrup, orange zest, cinnamon, and cherries and heat 2 minutes. Place cheese on serving platter and top with pecan mixture. Serve warm.

Serving Suggestion: *Go ahead and serve this with your favorite crackers, cut veggies, bread, fruit, or just about anything! After you try it, let us know what you like best.*

Bread Bowl
Buffalo Chicken Dip

Forget wrestling with chicken wing bones or getting your TV remote all gooped up with Buffalo sauce! Now, there's an easier way to serve and enjoy this game day classic. What we love about cooking this in an air fryer is how crispy the bread bowl gets as the spicy, cheesy dip warms up within it. Serve it with celery sticks and bread chunks, and get ready for lots of dippin'!

Makes 1-½ cups

Ingredients

1 (6-inch) round rye or sourdough bread

1 cup shredded cooked chicken

1 cup shredded mozzarella cheese

½ cup chopped celery

½ (8-ounce) package cream cheese, softened

¼ cup blue cheese crumbles

¼ cup Buffalo wing sauce

Preparation

1 Cut top of bread to about ¼ of the way down; set top aside. Hollow out inside, leaving about ½-inch of bread around edges. Cut top, and bread that was removed from the inside, into 1-inch cubes and set aside.

2 In a large bowl, combine all ingredients except bread; mix well. Spoon into prepared bread bowl. Preheat air fryer to 360 degrees F.

3 Wrap bread bowl in aluminum foil and place in air fryer basket. Air-fry 20 minutes; unwrap and continue to cook 4 to 5 more minutes or until golden and heated through. Serve with reserved bread cubes for dipping.

Test Kitchen Tip: *If all the dip doesn't fit in the bowl, you can pop it in the fridge and reheat it in the microwave when the bread bowl is almost empty.*

Almost Famous Reuben Dip

Did you know one of the most famous deli sandwiches of all time is the Reuben? With corned beef, sauerkraut, and Swiss cheese layered on rye bread, and slathered with Russian dressing, it's easy to understand why. We challenged ourselves and combined all that goodness into a dip that's soon to be famous. Yup, it's that good!

Serves 12

Ingredients

1 (8-ounce) package cream cheese, softened

½ cup sour cream

1 (8-ounce) can sauerkraut, well drained and chopped

⅓ pound sliced deli corned beef, chopped

1 cup (4-ounces) shredded Swiss cheese

1 tablespoon finely chopped onion

2 tablespoons ketchup

2 tablespoons spicy brown mustard

1 (16-ounce) package cocktail rye bread

Preparation

1 Coat a 3-cup baking dish or foil pan with cooking spray. (Make sure that it fits into your basket before filling it.)

2 In large bowl, combine all ingredients except rye bread; mix well and spoon into baking dish. Cover with aluminum foil, making sure to wrap the edges firmly, so the foil doesn't blow off during cooking.

3 Preheat air fryer to 350 degrees F. Place baking dish in air fryer basket and air-fry 15 minutes. Remove foil and continue to cook 5 to 6 more minutes or until top is golden and center is heated through. Serve warm with cocktail rye bread.

The "Everything" Munchie Mix

We think you're going to go nuts over this simple, but addictive, snack mix. Basically, it has everything in it, but the kitchen sink. After our team taste-tested this, they not only loved it, they couldn't wait to get the recipe, so that they could make it at home. And although we spell out what we think makes a great mix, feel free to add or subtract to it to make this your very own.

Makes 5 cups

Ingredients

1 cup oven-toasted corn cereal

1 cup miniature pretzel twists

1 cup cheese crackers

1 cup whole cashews

1 tablespoon vegetable oil

½ teaspoon onion powder

½ teaspoon garlic powder

¼ teaspoon cayenne pepper

1 cup banana chips

½ cup dried cranberries

Preparation

1 Preheat air fryer to 380 degrees F.

2 In a large bowl, combine cereal, pretzels, cheese crackers, and cashews.

3 In a small bowl, combine oil, onion powder, garlic powder, and cayenne pepper; mix well. Pour seasoned oil over cereal mixture; toss until thoroughly coated. Place in air fryer basket.

4 Air-fry 5 minutes, shaking basket 2 to 3 times during cooking process. (This way everything cooks evenly.) Add banana chips and cranberries; shake basket. Remove snack mix from air fryer, place in serving bowl, and let cool slightly. Serve warm or store in an airtight container until ready to munch on.

Test Kitchen Tip: *To make this for a crowd, just double the recipe and cook it in batches. There's nothing as crowd-pleasin' as fresh-from-the-oven … oops, we meant air fryer, munchie mix!*

Simple Sandwiches, Pizzas, & Breads

3-in-1 Grilled Cheese

Grilled cheese sandwiches are already one of the most popular sandwiches ever. But Patty, who heads up our Test Kitchen, found a way to make them even better. Not only did she add macaroni and cheese to these sandwiches (yes, we said macaroni and cheese), but she also loaded them up with flavorful, pulled pork. As you can imagine, we were all eager to taste-test them. The results were absolutely mind-blowing!

Makes 3

Ingredients

1 (12-ounce) package frozen macaroni and cheese

¾ cup shredded mozzarella cheese

6 slices sourdough bread

1 (16-ounce) container refrigerated barbecue pork

3 tablespoons butter, softened

Preparation

1 Microwave macaroni and cheese according to package directions. Let cool for 5 minutes, then stir in mozzarella cheese.

2 Place 3 slices of bread on a work surface. Evenly divide macaroni and cheese mixture on each slice of bread. Top each with ½ cup pork then with the remaining bread slices. Evenly spread half the butter on tops of sandwiches.

3 Preheat air fryer to 380 degrees F.

4 Coat air fryer basket with cooking spray. Working in batches, place a sandwich in basket, butter-side down, and spread top with some of remaining butter. Air-fry 7 to 8 minutes, turn over, and cook 3 to 4 more minutes or until heated through and golden. Repeat with remaining sandwiches. When last sandwich is done, place first 2 back in for 1 minute to warm up.

Bistro-Style Roast Beef Sliders

These have a high likelihood of becoming your new go-to dinner sandwich. They're easy to make, and have a real gourmet taste to them. That's because they're made with easy-to-find special-tasting ingredients, like a garlic herb spread and crusty ciabatta bread. Plus there's the peppery arugula and the thinly sliced roast beef. When these come together, they're positively heavenly.

Makes 4

Ingredients

4 slider-sized ciabatta rolls, cut in half

1 tablespoon olive oil

2 teaspoons chopped fresh rosemary

Sea salt for sprinkling

2 tablespoons refrigerated garlic herb spread

½ pound thinly sliced deli roast beef

½ cup arugula

Preparation

1 Preheat air fryer to 380 degrees F.

2 Brush tops of rolls with olive oil. Sprinkle evenly with rosemary and salt. Coat air fryer basket with cooking spray and place tops in basket, cut-side down. Air-fry 3 minutes or until lightly golden. Remove from basket and set aside.

3 Spread cut-side of bottoms with garlic herb spread; place in basket and cook 2 minutes or until warmed. Remove from basket, then top evenly with roast beef and arugula. Place tops of rolls on sandwiches and serve.

Open-Faced Thanksgiving Sandwiches

There's no reason to wait until next November to satisfy your cravings for Thanksgiving dinner! You can have these open-faced sandwiches on your table in just about 15 minutes. They're loaded with some of your favorite Thanksgiving Day foods, including stuffing, turkey, cranberry sauce, and gravy. Your cravings don't stand a chance!

Serves 2

Ingredients

¼ cup cranberry sauce

¼ cup mayonnaise

2 kaiser rolls, cut in half

8 slices (about 6 ounces) cooked turkey (see Tip)

1 cup prepared stuffing

¼ cup gravy, warmed

Preparation

1 Preheat air fryer to 360 degrees F.

2 In a small bowl, combine cranberry sauce and mayonnaise; mix well.

3 Place rolls cut-side up on a work surface and evenly spread cranberry mayo on each. (Since these will be open-faced sandwiches, we'll be using the tops and bottoms the same.) Evenly pile on turkey, then top with stuffing.

4 Wrap each in foil and place 2 in air fryer basket. Air-fry 5 minutes. Unwrap and cook 3 to 4 more minutes or until heated through. Repeat with remaining sandwiches. Spoon gravy over stuffing and serve.

Test Kitchen Tip: *To get that true Thanksgiving feeling, we recommend asking the deli to slice the turkey a bit thicker. If you ever have leftover turkey, pop that into the freezer, so you can make this whenever you get a hankering for it. As for the stuffing, we like to use the quick-cooking stovetop kind.*

Overstuffed Monte Cristos

There's a reason why many of us rarely make Monte Cristo sandwiches at home. Fact is, we just don't want to go through all the hassle that comes with deep frying. Well all that has changed, thanks to the much easier and healthier method of air frying. And for those of you who've never had a Monte Cristo before – we like to describe it as French toast meets overstuffed deli sandwich.

Serves 2

Ingredients

2 tablespoons yellow mustard

1 tablespoon honey

4 (1-inch-thick) slices challah bread

¼ pound thinly sliced deli turkey

¼ pound thinly sliced deli ham

4 (1-ounce) slices Swiss cheese

2 eggs

¼ cup milk

Preparation

1 Preheat air fryer to 380 degrees F. In a small bowl, combine yellow mustard and honey.

2 Place 2 slices of bread on a work surface and spread with honey mustard. Evenly layer on turkey, ham, and cheese. Spread 1 side of each slice of remaining bread with honey mustard and place on top of cheese.

3 In a medium bowl, whisk eggs and milk until well combined.

4 Coat air fryer basket with cooking spray. Dip sandwiches, one at a time, into egg mixture, coating completely. Place in basket, one at a time, and air-fry 4 minutes. Turn sandwich over and cook 3 to 4 more minutes or until golden and cheese is melted. Repeat with remaining sandwich. After second sandwich is done, place the first one back in for 1 minute to warm up.

Serving Suggestion: *Keep things traditional by serving your Monte Cristos with a dusting of powdered sugar and a side of warm strawberry or raspberry jam. It's delicious!*

Simply-the-Best Tuna Melts

Before setting out to make this book we never thought of making a tuna melt in an air fryer. But now we're so glad we did. These are simply the best! From the perfectly toasted English muffin to the flavorful tuna mixture, it's all good. And of course, who can forget about the melted cheese that brings all the goodness together? This tuna melt is a dream come true.

Makes 4

Ingredients

1 (12-ounce) can tuna, drained and flaked

½ cup mayonnaise

1 stalk celery, sliced

¼ teaspoon onion powder

¼ teaspoon black pepper

2 English muffins, split in half

Cooking spray

2 plum tomatoes, cut into 8 slices total

4 slices Muenster cheese

Preparation

1 Preheat air fryer to 380 degrees F.

2 In a medium bowl, combine tuna, mayonnaise, celery, onion powder, and pepper; mix well.

3 Coat air fryer basket with cooking spray. Spray tops of English muffins with cooking spray; place all four halves in basket and air-fry 2 minutes or until toasted.

4 Remove from basket and spread equal amounts of tuna mixture on each English muffin half. Top each with 2 slices of tomato and a slice of cheese.

5 Working in batches, place in basket, 2 at a time, and cook 3 minutes or until cheese is melted and sandwich is heated through. Serve immediately.

Meatball & Ricotta Personal Pizzas

These pizzas are so good we challenge you to try a blind taste test. If your gang thinks you bought these from a pizza shop, then you know you've won! We love how the dough gets crispy around the edges, but still tastes light and fresh. There's also something to be said about the combination of ricotta with mozzarella; it's amazing! Then there are the meatballs; hearty and full of flavor. This is definitely worth a "Mamma mia!"

Makes 4

Ingredients

1 pound store-bought pizza dough, kept at room temperature for 30 to 60 minutes to let rise

1 tablespoon olive oil

½ cup pizza sauce

½ cup shredded mozzarella cheese

½ cup ricotta cheese

8 small frozen Italian meatballs, thawed and cut in half

Preparation

1 Place a 4-inch-wide foil sling (see page ix) in air fryer basket. Preheat air fryer to 390 degrees F.

2 Coat sling and basket with cooking spray. Cut pizza dough into 4 quarters. Using your fingers, form dough into 6-inch circles. Using a fork, prick dough about 10 times. Brush both sides of dough lightly with oil. Place 1 piece of dough in basket. Air-fry 4 minutes, turn over, and continue to cook 1 to 2 more minutes or until golden. Remove crust and set aside. Repeat with remaining dough.

3 Spread 2 tablespoons pizza sauce over each crust. Sprinkle evenly with mozzarella cheese. Top each with 3 spoonfuls of ricotta cheese and 4 meatball halves. Place one pizza at a time on sling in basket. Cook 2 to 3 minutes or until heated through. Remove pizza using foil sling. Repeat with remaining pizzas.

Serving Suggestion: *Finish each slice with some slivered fresh basil and, if you like things on the spicier side, a shake or two of crushed red pepper. Yum!*

Pizzeria-Style Strombolis

You don't need to leave your kitchen to make a pizzeria-worthy stromboli. These "bake" perfectly in your air fryer. You see, the air fryer allows hot air to circulate all around the stromboli, which results in a crunchy-on-the-outside, yet tender-on-the-inside crust. Plus, there's all the molten meat and cheese filling too. In the end, you get to enjoy a really authentic-tasting stromboli.

Makes 4

Ingredients

1 (11-ounce) can refrigerated thin crust pizza dough

16 slices thinly sliced deli salami

1 cup spinach leaves

½ cup sliced roasted red peppers

8 slices provolone cheese

4 tablespoons Italian dressing

Cooking spray

1 teaspoon Italian seasoning, divided

Parmesan cheese for sprinkling

Preparation

1   Preheat air fryer to 350 degrees F. Unroll pizza dough on a cutting board and cut into 4 equal-sized rectangles.

2   Layer each piece of dough evenly with salami, spinach, red peppers, provolone cheese, and 1 tablespoon Italian dressing. Starting at the long edge of dough, roll up jelly roll-style. Spray top of each with cooking spray, then evenly sprinkle with Italian seasoning and Parmesan cheese.

3   Coat air fryer basket with cooking spray. Place 2 strombolis in basket and air-fry 9 to 10 minutes or until golden brown. Repeat with remaining strombolis. After the second 2 are done, place first 2 back in for 1 minute to warm up.

Ready-When-You-Are BBQ Hawaiian Pizzas

This recipe is perfect for those nights when everyone needs to eat dinner at a different time. Between after school sports, PTA meetings, and all the running around, it's nice to know you can whip up a fresh, tropical pizza in minutes. We suggest baking the crusts and assembling the pizzas ahead of time, so whenever your troops come home, you can pop one of these in the air fryer and have it ready in no time.

Makes 4

Ingredients

1 (13.8-ounce) can refrigerated pizza dough

Cooking spray

1 cup shredded mozzarella cheese

1 cup diced cooked chicken

1 (8-ounce) can pineapple tidbits, drained well

¼ cup diced red onion

½ cup barbecue sauce

1 tablespoon chopped fresh cilantro

Preparation

1 Preheat air fryer to 390 degrees F.

2 Unroll dough onto a cutting board. Cut into 4 equal rectangles. Lightly spray tops with cooking spray. Coat air fryer basket with cooking spray. Place one dough rectangle in basket. Air-fry 3 to 4 minutes or until light golden. Turn over, lightly spray with cooking spray, and continue to cook 2 to 3 more minutes or until golden. Remove crust from basket and set aside. Repeat process with remaining dough rectangles.

3 Place a 4-inch-wide foil sling (see page ix) in basket (be careful as basket will be hot). Evenly layer each crust with mozzarella cheese, chicken, pineapple, and red onion.

4 Place one pizza at a time on sling in basket and cook 2 to 3 minutes or until heated through. Remove pizza using foil sling; drizzle with barbecue sauce and sprinkle with cilantro. Repeat with remaining pizzas. Serve warm.

Beefed-Up Wet Burritos

You're gonna need a knife and fork to conquer these deliciously-messy, wet burritos. Not only are they stuffed with beef, beans, and lots of veggies, but once they're air-fried, we smother 'em in cheese and a flavorful enchilada sauce. They're so darn good, you might find yourself saying, "Ay, caramba!" Grab a handful of napkins and dig in!

Makes 4

Ingredients

1 pound ground beef

⅓ cup chopped onion

⅓ cup diced green bell pepper

1 (1-ounce) packet taco seasoning mix

2 tablespoons water

½ cup refried beans

4 (10-inch) flour tortillas

2 cups shredded lettuce

1 cup chopped tomatoes

1 cup shredded pepper jack cheese, divided

Cooking spray

1 (10-ounce) can enchilada sauce

Preparation

1 Preheat air fryer to 370 degrees F.

2 In a large skillet over medium-high heat, cook beef, onion, and bell pepper 5 to 6 minutes or until beef is no longer pink. Drain liquid. Stir in taco seasoning mix and water; cook 3 minutes. Remove from heat and set aside.

3 Spread about 2 tablespoons of refried beans evenly onto each tortilla. Spoon ½ cup beef mixture down center of each tortilla and top with a layer of lettuce, tomatoes, and 2 tablespoons cheese. Fold edge closest to you over filling, fold in sides, and roll up burrito-style (see photo).

4 Coat air fryer basket with cooking spray. Place 2 burritos seam-side down in basket. Spray tops with cooking spray. Air-fry 7 to 8 minutes or until golden, turn over, and spray with cooking spray. Continue to cook 2 to 3 more minutes or until golden. Repeat with remaining 2 burritos.

5 Meanwhile, in a small saucepan over low heat, heat enchilada sauce until warm. Spoon sauce over burritos and sprinkle with remaining cheese. Serve immediately.

1-2-3 Mayo Rolls

All right, you have dinner planned out, the salad is made and – oops! – you forgot about the rolls! Sure, you can run to the store and pick up a loaf of bread made hours ago (if there's still any left) or you can make these. With only 3 ingredients and the help of your air fryer, you can have bakery-fresh rolls on the table in no time. Just make sure you don't forget the butter, 'cause these are best when slathered with lots of it.

Makes 7

Ingredients

1-½ cups self-rising flour

¾ cup milk

3 tablespoons mayonnaise

Preparation

1 Preheat air fryer to 350 degrees F. Coat 7 foil muffin cup liners with cooking spray. (See note.)

2 In a medium bowl, combine flour, milk, and mayonnaise; mix well. Spoon evenly into liners. Carefully place in air fryer basket and arrange so they are evenly spaced apart.

3 Air-fry 7 to 8 minutes or until a toothpick inserted in center comes out clean and tops are golden brown. Serve warm.

Did You Know? *Foil muffin cup liners are different than paper muffin liners as they're designed to be used without a muffin tin. That makes these perfect for this recipe!*

Cinnamon-Glazed Sweet Potato Biscuits

These sweet potato biscuits made their first appearance during one of our holiday TV segments. To make them work for this cookbook, we had to scale things down. After all, the original recipe made a boatload of biscuits! After many attempts, we finally got it right. Now you can make just enough of these delicate biscuits for the holidays or any night of the week. Don't forget to be generous with the glaze!

Makes 6

Ingredients

1 (2.5-ounce) jar sweet potatoes baby food

¼ cup milk

¼ cup granulated sugar

1 egg, beaten

1 tablespoon butter, melted

1-½ cups self-rising flour

½ teaspoon baking powder

¼ teaspoon salt

¼ cup vegetable shortening

CINNAMON GLAZE

1 tablespoon butter, melted

1 teaspoon brown sugar

⅛ teaspoon ground cinnamon

Preparation

1. Preheat air fryer to 350 degrees F.

2. In a small bowl, combine sweet potatoes, milk, granulated sugar, egg, and 1 tablespoon butter; mix well.

3. Coat air fryer basket with cooking spray. In a medium bowl, combine flour, baking powder, and salt. Using 2 knives or a pastry cutter, cut shortening into flour mixture. Pour sweet potato mixture into flour mixture and mix until just combined.

4. Spoon 3 large spoonfuls of the dough (each about the size of a golf ball) into basket, leaving space around each. (They will expand as they bake.)

5. Air-fry 10 to 11 minutes or until golden. Repeat with remaining batter. When the second batch is done, you can place the first ones back in for 1 minute to warm up. Meanwhile, in a small bowl, combine all Cinnamon Glaze ingredients. Brush biscuit tops with glaze and serve warm.

Cheesy Scallion Crescent Rolls

All of us in the Test Kitchen love when we can take an everyday off-the-shelf ingredient and turn it into something that's extra special. (It's sort of our job!) Thanks to air fryers, we can have cheesy-good crescent rolls on the table in about 5 minutes. If only everything in life were this easy!

Makes 8

Ingredients

1 (8-ounce) can refrigerated crescent rolls

½ cup finely shredded cheddar cheese

¼ cup chopped scallions

Cooking spray

1 teaspoon sesame seeds

Preparation

1 Preheat air fryer to 350 degrees F.

2 Unroll dough and separate into 8 triangles. Sprinkle each triangle evenly with cheese and scallions. Starting at the shortest side of the triangle (not the point), roll-up each piece of dough, then slightly bend each into a crescent shape. Lightly spray top of each with cooking spray and sprinkle with sesame seeds.

3 Coat air fryer basket with cooking spray. In batches, if necessary, place rolls in basket, making sure not to overcrowd. (They will expand as they cook.) Air-fry 4 to 5 minutes or until they puff up and turn golden. Serve warm.

Homemade Sourdough Croutons

Really good salads start with fresh ingredients, so why shouldn't we take care to finish them off the same way too? These croutons can be made in minutes and will add lots of crunch and flavor to every bite. Not only do they make great salad toppers, but they can be used in your favorite soups too.

Makes 3-½ cups

Ingredients

½ pound day-old sourdough bread, cut into 1-inch chunks (about 3-½ cups)

2 tablespoons vegetable oil

2 tablespoons dry ranch salad dressing and seasoning mix

Preparation

1 Preheat air fryer to 380 degrees F.

2 Place bread chunks in a medium bowl. Add oil and ranch mix; toss until evenly coated.

3 Coat air fryer basket with cooking spray. Place bread chunks in basket. Air-fry 2 minutes, shake basket so croutons get tossed around a bit, then continue to cook 2 to 3 more minutes or until golden and crispy.

4 Let cool. Serve immediately or store in an airtight container until ready to use.

Pleasing Poultry

Snap Cracklin' Parmesan Chicken

Over the years we've breaded chicken with just about everything you can think of. We've given chicken a Bavarian flair using a pretzel crust, a South-of-the-Border twist by breading it with crushed tortilla chips, and so on and so on. Now we're changing things up again by dipping chicken breasts in Thousand Island dressing before coating them with crushed rice cereal and Parmesan cheese. It might sound like an odd combo, but rest assured, it's a tasty one.

Makes 2

Ingredients

2 boneless, skinless chicken breasts

Salt for sprinkling

Black pepper for sprinkling

2 tablespoons all-purpose flour

⅓ cup Thousand Island dressing

1 cup crispy rice cereal, coarsely crushed

¼ cup grated Parmesan cheese

Preparation

1 Preheat air fryer to 350 degrees F.

2 Sprinkle chicken evenly with salt and pepper.

3 Place flour in a shallow dish. Place dressing in another shallow dish. In a third shallow dish, combine crushed cereal and Parmesan cheese; mix well.

4 Dip chicken in flour, followed by dressing, then cereal mixture, coating both sides evenly. Press coating firmly onto chicken, so it doesn't blow off in the air fryer.

5 Coat air fryer basket with cooking spray. Place both chicken breasts in basket making sure not to overlap. Air-fry 8 minutes, turn over, and continue cooking 8 to 9 more minutes or until no pink remains in chicken and crust is golden.

Good for You: *Just think how much healthier this dish is when cooked in an air fryer rather than deep frying it, in order to get that crispy coating. We love all that air fryers can do for us!*

Bacon-Wrapped Tropical Chicken

We haven't met anyone who doesn't love these. Here in the Test Kitchen, we feel that just about everything is better with bacon. That's why we took some plump chicken tenders and wrapped each one in bacon before basting them with a mouthwatering, pineapple-brown sugar glaze. These tenders are smoky with a tasty, tropical touch that's sure to become a family favorite.

Makes 8

Ingredients

½ cup pineapple preserves

2 tablespoons brown sugar

8 boneless, skinless chicken tenders (about 2 pounds)

Salt for sprinkling

Black pepper for sprinkling

8 slices bacon

Preparation

1 In a small saucepan over low heat, melt pineapple preserves with brown sugar, stirring occasionally; set aside.

2 Preheat air fryer to 400 degrees F.

3 Sprinkle chicken tenders evenly with salt and pepper. Wrap a slice of bacon around each tender, slightly overlapping as you go.

4 Coat air fryer basket with cooking spray and add 2 tablespoons water to pan. Working in batches, place bacon-wrapped chicken in basket, making sure not to overcrowd. Air-fry 7 minutes, then turn over and brush with pineapple glaze. Continue to cook 5 to 6 more minutes or until chicken is no longer pink in center and glaze starts to caramelize.

Good for You: *The air fryer basket allows the bacon fat (along with some of the calories, and cholesterol) to drip away. That way we end up with the crispy crunchy bacon we love, and not all the guilt.*

So Easy
Chicken Parmesan

Have you ever picked up a cookbook and found yourself feeling overwhelmed by instructions that are pages long? How about those cookbooks that call for several ingredients you can't pronounce or can't find anywhere in your supermarket? By now, you've probably realized that you'll never run into that problem with a Mr. Food Test Kitchen cookbook. Just take a look at this recipe – it's so easy for you to make this Italian restaurant favorite at home (and it's amazing!).

Makes 2

Ingredients

½ cup plain bread crumbs

1 tablespoon Italian seasoning

1 teaspoon garlic powder

1 egg

1 tablespoon water

2 boneless, skinless chicken breasts

Salt for sprinkling

Black pepper for sprinkling

½ cup spaghetti sauce

¼ cup shredded mozzarella cheese

Preparation

1 In a shallow dish, combine bread crumbs, Italian seasoning, and garlic powder. In another shallow dish, whisk egg and water. Evenly sprinkle both sides of chicken with salt and pepper.

2 Preheat air fryer to 350 degrees F.

3 Dip chicken into egg mixture, then into bread crumb mixture, coating both sides completely. Gently pat bread crumbs onto chicken so coating doesn't blow off in the air fryer.

4 Coat air fryer basket with cooking spray. Place chicken in basket. Air-fry 7 minutes, turn over, and continue to cook 4 to 5 more minutes or until no pink remains in chicken and breading is golden.

5 Spoon sauce over chicken and sprinkle with cheese. Cook an additional 1 to 2 minutes or until cheese is melted. Mangia!

Weeknight Chicken Milanese

This dish is said to have originated in the Italian city of Milan (must be where "Milanese" comes from!). While it's traditionally made with veal, we wanted to lighten things up by using chicken. But just because it's lighter, doesn't mean it's less flavorful. Between the rich, bread crumb coating, the juicy chicken, and the fresh and tasty salad, there's so much to love!

Makes 2

Ingredients

1 (8-ounce) boneless, skinless chicken breast (see Tip)

¼ cup all-purpose flour

¼ teaspoon salt, divided

¼ teaspoon black pepper, divided

1 egg

2 tablespoons water

¾ cup seasoned panko bread crumbs

Cooking spray

2 cups mixed greens

Assorted salad toppings (like cherry tomatoes, sliced cucumber, etc.)

Italian vinaigrette for drizzling

Test Kitchen Tip: It seems like chicken breasts are getting bigger and bigger every day! That's good news for this recipe, since you want 'em big enough to be able to cut in half and pound thin.

Preparation

1 Place chicken breast on a cutting board and with a sharp knife, carefully cut chicken breast in half horizontally, so that you end up with 2 cutlets. Place each cutlet between 2 sheets of wax paper and, using the smooth side of a meat mallet, pound until each cutlet is about ¼-inch thick.

2 In a shallow dish, combine flour, ⅛ teaspoon salt and ⅛ teaspoon pepper. In another shallow dish, whisk together egg and water. Place bread crumbs in a third shallow dish.

3 Preheat air fryer to 380 degrees F. Sprinkle both sides of cutlets with remaining ⅛ teaspoon each of salt and pepper. Coat cutlets with seasoned flour, then dip into egg mixture, followed by bread crumbs. (Make sure you firmly pat on the bread crumbs, so that the crumbs really stick.)

4 Coat air fryer basket with cooking spray. Place 1 cutlet in basket and spray lightly with cooking spray. Air-fry 5 minutes, turn over, spray lightly with cooking spray and continue to cook 3 to 4 more minutes or until no pink remains in center and breading is crispy. Remove from basket and repeat with remaining cutlet.

5 When ready to serve, place chicken on a plate, then top evenly with mixed greens and salad fixin's. Drizzle with vinaigrette.

Super Stuffed Chicken Divan

Here's an idea! How about tonight, you surprise your family and friends with a chicken dish that's brimming with goodness? Not only will they be excited about their dinner being coated in their favorite cheese crackers, but once they cut into it, they're going to be even more thrilled! After all, who doesn't love an ooey-gooey, cheddar and broccoli filling? Although this one looks like it takes a lot of work, it's absolutely weeknight easy.

Makes 4

Ingredients

4 (4-ounce) boneless, skinless chicken breasts

Salt for sprinkling

Black pepper for sprinkling

½ cup frozen chopped broccoli, thawed and patted dry

¼ cup diced cheddar cheese (about 2 ounces)

1 tablespoon bacon bits

1 cup crushed cheese crackers

Cooking spray

Test Kitchen Tip: *Depending on the size of the chicken breasts and your air fryer, you may have to cook these in a couple of batches.*

Preparation

1   Place chicken on a cutting board, cover with wax paper, and, with the smooth side of a meat mallet, flatten chicken until ¼-inch thick. Sprinkle with salt and pepper.

2   In a medium bowl, combine broccoli, cheese, and bacon bits; mix well. Evenly divide broccoli mixture onto each breast. Beginning with the shortest end, roll each chicken breast jelly roll-style, making sure to tuck in the sides and secure with a few toothpicks. (You don't want all that cheesy goodness to ooze out while they cook!)

3   Preheat air fryer to 350 degrees F. In a shallow dish, place crushed crackers. Generously spray each chicken breast with cooking spray and coat with crushed crackers, pressing lightly to secure.

4   Coat air fryer basket with cooking spray and place chicken in basket, seam-side down. Lightly spray tops with cooking spray one last time, and air-fry 20 to 22 minutes or until no pink remains in chicken. Remove toothpicks and enjoy.

Better-Than-Ever Honey Garlic Chicken

Yes you can make honey garlic chicken in an air fryer! In fact, cooking it this way means less fat and calories (when compared to the traditional deep-fried method). Plus the chicken comes out super juicy and has a nice bite to it. Our version of this Asian-inspired entrée features your favorite classic sauce and chunks of red peppers for even more deliciousness. Serve it over rice and sprinkle on some scallions to complete your meal.

Serves 2

Ingredients

1 tablespoon sesame seeds

1 teaspoon vegetable oil

1 red bell pepper, cut into 1-inch chunks

1 tablespoon soy sauce

1 tablespoon plus 1 teaspoon cornstarch, divided

½ cup honey

2 cloves garlic, minced

1 tablespoon all-purpose flour

½ teaspoon paprika

¼ teaspoon salt

1 pound boneless, skinless chicken breasts, cut into 1-inch chunks

Cooking spray

Preparation

1 In a medium skillet over medium-high heat, toast sesame seeds until golden, stirring occasionally. (Be careful, once they start browning they go quickly!) Remove from skillet and set aside.

2 In the same skillet over medium heat, heat oil until hot; sauté red pepper 2 minutes. In a small bowl, whisk soy sauce and 1 teaspoon cornstarch until smooth. Add honey and garlic to the skillet, along with the soy sauce mixture, and cook 3 to 4 minutes or until sauce begins to thicken. Set aside.

3 Preheat air fryer to 400 degrees F.

4 In a medium bowl, combine remaining 1 tablespoon cornstarch, the flour, paprika, and salt; mix well. Add chicken and toss until evenly coated. Coat air fryer basket with cooking spray. Place chicken in basket, lightly coat with cooking spray, and air-fry 5 minutes, shaking basket halfway through cooking. Continue to cook 3 more minutes or until no longer pink in center.

5 Add chicken to honey garlic sauce and simmer about 1 minute or until heated through. Serve immediately topped with toasted sesame seeds.

Chicken & Veggie Shepherd's Pies

Now before you get all wound up, we know that traditional shepherd's pie is made with lamb; however, we thought it would be an affordable and tasty option to make this with chicken. As for the mashed potato topping, no worries, we didn't skimp on it. After all, it's what makes this so darn comforting. Now go on and be comforted!

Serves 4

Ingredients

2 (6-ounce) boneless, skinless chicken breasts

¼ teaspoon salt, plus extra for sprinkling

¼ teaspoon black pepper, plus extra for sprinkling

1 (12-ounce) jar chicken gravy

1-½ cups frozen mixed vegetables, thawed

½ teaspoon onion powder

2 cups prepared mashed potatoes, warmed slightly

2 tablespoons butter, melted

Test Kitchen Tip: To help you get the crocks in and out of the air fryer basket, try using a foil sling. Check out page ix to learn more about how handy these are.

Preparation

1 Preheat air fryer to 350 degrees F.

2 Coat air fryer basket with cooking spray. Sprinkle chicken with salt and pepper, place in basket, and air-fry 5 minutes. Turn chicken over and continue to cook 5 to 6 more minutes or until no pink remains in center. Remove to a cutting board, let cool slightly, and cut into ½-inch chunks.

3 Meanwhile, in a skillet over medium heat, combine gravy, vegetables, onion powder, ¼ teaspoon salt, and ¼ teaspoon pepper. Cook 5 to 7 minutes or until heated through. Stir in chicken and spoon mixture evenly into 4 (1-cup) oven-proof crocks or ramekins.

4 Top each crock with ½ cup mashed potatoes and drizzle melted butter on top.

5 Increase temperature of air fryer to 400 degrees F. Working with two at a time, place crocks in basket and cook 6 to 7 minutes or until heated through and tops are golden. Repeat with remaining two crocks.

Crispy Chicken Fries

No need to head to the drive-thru to get your hands on our Crispy Chicken Fries. Although these look like traditional fast food fries, don't let them fool ya! These are made using boneless chicken breasts that are cut into strips and then air-fried to perfection. These are so good, you could say they're fit for a king (wink, wink).

Serves 4

Ingredients

1 pound boneless, skinless chicken breasts

2 cups panko bread crumbs

1 teaspoon garlic powder

½ teaspoon onion powder

1 teaspoon salt

½ teaspoon black pepper

2 eggs

½ cup all-purpose flour

Cooking spray

Test Kitchen Tip: *If you want these to look like fries, make sure you lay them out so they're straight.*

Preparation

1 Place chicken breasts on a cutting board and with a sharp knife, carefully cut each in half horizontally. Then cut each half into long, thin strips, resembling french fries.

2 In a shallow dish, combine bread crumbs, garlic powder, onion powder, salt, and pepper; mix well. In another shallow dish, beat eggs. Place flour in a third shallow dish.

3 Preheat air fryer to 380 degrees F. Working with a few strips at a time, dredge in flour, dip in egg, then coat with bread crumb mixture, pressing the breading firmly onto each strip.

4 Coat air fryer basket with cooking spray. Working in batches, place a layer of strips into basket, being careful not to overcrowd. (See Tip.) Lightly spray strips with cooking spray.

5 Air-fry 4 minutes, shake basket (to ensure everything cooks evenly), and continue to cook 2 minutes or until chicken is no longer pink in center and coating is crispy. Repeat with remaining strips. Once all the "fries" are cooked, you can place them all back in the basket and heat for about 1 minute to warm up.

Greek Isles "Roasted" Chicken

Did you know you can roast chicken and meat in an air fryer? The high heat and convection fan create the perfect environment for searing chicken and beef. The results are moist and juicy! And since the air fryer basket and pan are dishwasher safe; clean-up is a breeze. We can't think of a better recipe than this one for you to put your air fryer's "roasting" skills to the test!

Serves 4

Ingredients

2 tablespoons olive oil

2 teaspoons lemon juice

1 teaspoon dried oregano

½ teaspoon garlic powder

½ teaspoon salt

¼ teaspoon black pepper

2 pounds boneless, skinless chicken thighs

1 (2.25-ounce) can sliced black olives, drained well

½ cup crumbled feta cheese

Preparation

1 In a large bowl, combine oil, lemon juice, oregano, garlic powder, salt, and pepper; mix well. Add chicken and toss until evenly coated. Cover and refrigerate at least 1 hour.

2 Preheat air fryer to 380 degrees F.

3 Coat air fryer basket with cooking spray. Place chicken in basket. Air-fry 17 to 18 minutes or until no longer pink in center. Serve topped with sliced olives and crumbled feta.

Serving Suggestion: *Round out your meal by serving this over orzo tossed with some olive oil, chopped parsley, and a bit of salt and pepper. Simple and tasty!*

Pop Pop
Popcorn Chicken

Do you think it's just a coincidence that KFC® started with a Colonel (as in Sanders) and popcorn (as in popcorn chicken) also starts with a kernel? (We know their popcorn chicken doesn't actually start from kernels – we're just having some fun!) Talking about things that are fun, our made-from-scratch popcorn chicken is super fun to make and even more fun to eat. Put out a bowl of your favorite dipping sauce and go to town.

Makes about 40 pieces

Ingredients

2 boneless, skinless chicken breasts

½ teaspoon salt

¼ teaspoon black pepper

¼ cup all-purpose flour

2 eggs

½ cup plain bread crumbs

1 teaspoon poultry seasoning

½ teaspoon onion powder

½ teaspoon garlic powder

¼ teaspoon paprika

Cooking spray

¼ cup yellow mustard

3 tablespoons honey

Preparation

1 In a food processor, process chicken until it's finely ground. Add salt and pepper and pulse to combine. Form chicken into 40 irregularly shaped pieces, so they resemble popcorn.

2 Place flour in a shallow dish. In another shallow dish, whisk eggs. In a third shallow dish combine bread crumbs, poultry seasoning, onion powder, garlic powder, and paprika; mix well.

3 Preheat air fryer to 360 degrees F.

4 Coat air fryer basket with cooking spray. Dredge chicken pieces in flour, then egg, and finally in bread crumb mixture. Place half the breaded pieces in basket. Lightly spray with cooking spray. Air-fry 4 minutes. Shake basket to turn chicken pieces, and lightly spray again with cooking spray. Continue to cook 3 to 4 more minutes or until no pink remains in center and breading is golden brown. Repeat with remaining chicken pieces.

5 Meanwhile, in a small bowl, combine mustard and honey; mix well. Serve hot popcorn chicken with honey mustard mixture.

Chicken Taco Salad Bowl

With the help of your air fryer you can make this trendy restaurant salad at home. It's loaded with yummy seasoned chicken and a bunch of taco salad fixin's. But what makes this salad unique is that it's served in an edible tortilla bowl. So the next time you're craving a fancy taco salad, skip going to a restaurant and break out the air fryer!

Makes 2 Salads

Ingredients

2 (10-inch) flour tortillas

Cooking spray

SEASONING BLEND

1 teaspoon chili powder

½ teaspoon ground cumin

½ teaspoon onion powder

½ teaspoon salt

¼ teaspoon black pepper

1 (6-ounce) boneless, skinless chicken breast

2 cups chopped romaine lettuce

½ cup black beans, rinsed and drained

½ cup frozen corn, thawed

¼ cup chopped tomato

½ cup shredded cheddar cheese

1 tablespoon chopped red onion

1 avocado, pitted and cut into chunks

Preparation

1 Preheat air fryer to 360 degrees F. Lightly spray both sides of tortillas with cooking spray. Place one tortilla in air fryer basket so that it forms a bowl. (How high it comes up the sides will vary based on the size of your air fryer. The one in the photo was made in a 3.4-quart air fryer.) Place a foil ring inside the tortilla, to help it hold its shape. Air-fry 4 minutes, remove foil ring, turn tortilla bowl over, and continue to cook 2 minutes or until crispy. Repeat with second tortilla.

2 Meanwhile, in a small bowl, combine Seasoning Blend ingredients; mix well. Sprinkle both sides of chicken with seasoning blend. Coat basket with cooking spray, place chicken in basket, and air-fry 12 to 13 minutes or until no longer pink in center. Let cool, then slice.

3 Divide lettuce evenly into tortilla bowls. Top evenly with black beans, corn, tomato, cheese, onion, avocado, and chicken. Drizzle with your favorite dressing. (We like ranch mixed with a bit of hot sauce for this salad.)

Truly Southern "Fried" Chicken

Let us introduce you to a recipe that really shines when "fried" in our air fryer. When we started out to make this, our goal was to create "fried" chicken that tasted like it was deep-fried, yet made in an air fryer. We're happy to say we did it. One bite and you too will be convinced The breading is crispy, the meat is juicy, and the fat and calories are way less than if it was deep-fried.

Serves 4

Ingredients

⅓ cup milk

1 egg

1 (2-½ to 3-pound) chicken, cut into 8 pieces

1-¼ cups all-purpose flour

1 teaspoon paprika

2 teaspoons salt

1 teaspoon black pepper

Cooking spray

Preparation

1 In a large bowl, combine milk and egg; mix well. Add chicken and toss to coat. In another large bowl, combine flour, paprika, salt, and pepper; mix well. Remove chicken from milk mixture and dredge it in flour mixture, coating completely. Then re-dip each chicken piece in milk and flour mixtures. (Yes, do this twice ... trust us.)

2 Preheat air fryer to 360 degrees F.

3 Coat air fryer basket with cooking spray. Working in batches, carefully place chicken in basket. Spray with cooking spray. Air-fry 12 minutes, turn chicken over, spray again, and continue to cook 12 to 14 more minutes or until chicken is no longer pink inside and coating is golden. Cover to keep warm. Repeat with remaining pieces.

Test Kitchen Tip: *Once all the chicken is cooked, and depending on the size of your air fryer, you may want to place all the cooked pieces back in the air fryer for a minute or so to heat them up.*

Summertime BBQ Drumsticks

We're always looking for ways to stretch our dollars. One place to start is in the meat case. Have you seen how affordable chicken drumsticks are by the pound? If you haven't, we suggest you pick some up the next time you're at the market, so you can give this recipe a try. While you're there, pick up an extra package of napkins — you'll need 'em!

Serves 3

Ingredients

BBQ SAUCE

1 cup ketchup

½ cup sweet and sour sauce

¼ cup firmly packed brown sugar

1 tablespoon white vinegar

3 tablespoons minced onion

1 tablespoon Worcestershire or steak sauce

2 tablespoons prepared mustard

2 pounds chicken drumsticks (about 6)

Preparation

1 To make BBQ sauce, in a medium bowl, combine ketchup, sweet and sour sauce, brown sugar, vinegar, onion, Worcestershire sauce, and mustard; mix well and set aside.

2 Preheat air fryer to 370 degrees F.

3 Coat air fryer basket with cooking spray. Place chicken in basket and air-fry 6 minutes. Turn chicken over and continue to cook 6 more minutes.

4 Brush chicken with sauce and continue to cook 5 more minutes. Turn chicken, brush with more sauce, and continue to cook 5 more minutes or until chicken is cooked through and sauce begins to caramelize.

Test Kitchen Tip: *To make this really taste like chicken right off the grill, increase the temperature to 400 degrees F after brushing it with sauce and cook for an extra minute or so, until the sauce just starts to char.*

Lemon Pepper Rotisserie Chicken

Every time we buy a rotisserie chicken and bring it back to the Test Kitchen we marvel at how juicy and flavorful it is. Now with the help of our air fryer, along with a really amazing spice blend and some fresh lemon, we're able to get those same results without leaving the kitchen. By the way, this chicken goes great with everything, so serve it with your family's favorite sides.

Serves 4

Ingredients

1 lemon

2 tablespoons vegetable oil

½ teaspoon garlic powder

½ teaspoon onion powder

1-½ teaspoons salt

½ teaspoon coarse black pepper

1 (2-½- to 3-pound) chicken

½ onion, cut into quarters

1 tablespoon water

Preparation

1 In a small bowl, zest lemon and set aside. Cut lemon in half and squeeze juice into another small bowl. Set the lemon halves aside. (They will get used later.)

2 In the bowl with the lemon zest, add half of lemon juice, the oil, garlic powder, onion powder, salt, and pepper; mix well. Pour over chicken and rub evenly over skin.

3 Now take one half of the juiced lemon and stuff it, along with the onion quarters, into the breast cavity. Using baker's twine, tie legs together. (This is called trussing.) Preheat air fryer to 340 degrees F.

4 Coat air fryer basket with cooking spray. Add remaining lemon juice (from the bowl) and 1 tablespoon water to air fryer pan. Place chicken breast-side up in basket and air-fry 20 minutes, along with the remaining lemon half that was already juiced.

5 Turn chicken over and continue to cook 20 more minutes. One last time, turn chicken over so breast is facing up and continue to cook 10 to 15 more minutes or until a meat thermometer inserted in thigh reaches 165 degrees F. Remove to a cutting board and let rest 5 minutes before carving.

Memphis-Style Chicken Wings

As you can see from the photo, these are no wimpy wings. For those times when "good" is just not good enough, we suggest whipping up a batch of these. What makes them extra-special is the Memphis-style dry rub followed by the lick-your-fingers-clean barbecue sauce. We do want to warn you that serving these on game day in front of the TV may result in red fingerprints on the arms of your couch. Just sayin'!

Serves 4

Ingredients

2-½ pounds fresh whole chicken wings (about 14 wings)

2 tablespoons smoked paprika

1 tablespoon light brown sugar

2 teaspoons ground cumin

1-½ teaspoons celery salt

1-½ teaspoons garlic powder

1 teaspoon dry mustard

1 tablespoon salt

½ teaspoon black pepper

½ teaspoon cayenne pepper

Cooking spray

1 cup Memphis-style barbecue sauce

Preparation

1 Preheat air fryer to 400 degrees F. Pat wings dry with paper towels and place in a large bowl.

2 In a small bowl, combine paprika, brown sugar, cumin, celery salt, garlic powder, dry mustard, salt, black pepper, and cayenne pepper; mix well. Rub mixture over wings until evenly coated.

3 Coat air fryer basket with cooking spray. Working in batches, place half the wings in basket and spray lightly with cooking spray. (It's okay if they're piled slightly, as long as the heat can get all around them.) Air-fry 6 minutes.

4 Turn wings over, making sure that the wings that are on the bottom make their way to the top. Spray lightly with cooking spray and continue to cook 6 more minutes. Turn wings over one more time and continue to cook 6 to 8 more minutes or until no pink remains in center and wings are crispy. Repeat with remaining wings.

5 Right before serving, drizzle wings with barbecue sauce and dig in.

Fuzzy Navel Cornish Hens

Have you ever had a Fuzzy Navel? No, we aren't talking about the lint you find in your belly button! A Fuzzy Navel is a wonderful cocktail made with orange juice and peach schnapps. In this recipe, we created a flavor-packed glaze, inspired by this famous cocktail, that you can slather on Cornish hens. Why Cornish hens? Well, we just love how each one is the perfect size for one person.

Serves 2

Ingredients

2 tablespoons vegetable oil

½ teaspoon salt

¼ teaspoon black pepper

2 Cornish hens, about 1 pound each, thawed if frozen

4 tablespoons peach schnapps, divided (see Tip)

1 tablespoon water

1 cup orange marmalade

So Many Options: If you prefer, you can use peach nectar instead of the peach schnapps.

Preparation

1 Preheat air fryer to 390 degrees F.

2 In a small bowl, combine oil, salt, and pepper; mix well. After rinsing the hens inside and out with cold water, pat dry with paper towels. Rub oil mixture over hens, coating completely. Using baker's twine, tie hens' legs together.

3 Coat air fryer basket with cooking spray. Add 1 tablespoon of peach schnapps and the water into air fryer pan. Place hens in basket breast-side up and air-fry 10 minutes.

4 Meanwhile, in a small saucepan over low heat, combine orange marmalade and remaining peach schnapps; heat just until marmalade is melted. Remove from heat.

5 Turn hens over and continue to cook 5 more minutes; brush with half the marmalade mixture and continue to cook 5 minutes. Turn hens over one more time (this time the breast should be up), and brush with remaining marmalade mixture. Continue to cook 5 to 6 more minutes or until a thermometer inserted into thigh reaches 165 degrees F and glaze is caramelized.

Chicken Sausage with Peppers & Onions

Long gone are the days of waiting for the county fair to roll into town, just so you can get your annual fix of sausage, peppers, and onions. Now you can get your fix as often as you'd like! Whether you enjoy these as is or piled high on a crusty roll, we bet each bite will have you smiling from ear to ear. The only thing missing is a funnel cake and a stuffed animal!

Serves 4

Ingredients

1 green bell pepper, cut into ½-inch strips

1 red bell pepper, cut into ½-inch strips

½ onion, cut into half moons

1 tablespoon vegetable oil

½ teaspoon garlic powder

½ teaspoon salt

¼ teaspoon black pepper

1 (12-ounce) package Italian-style cooked chicken sausage

Preparation

1 Preheat air fryer to 380 degrees F.

2 In a medium bowl, combine green and red bell pepper strips, onion, oil, garlic powder, salt, and black pepper; toss until evenly coated. Place in air fryer basket and air-fry 10 to 12 minutes or just until tender, shaking basket halfway through cooking, so they cook evenly. Remove to a bowl and cover to keep warm.

3 Cut 3 slits in each sausage (to prevent them from bursting during cooking), and place in basket. Air-fry 5 to 7 minutes or until heated through. Serve with peppers and onions.

Good for You: *If you haven't tried chicken sausage, we think you'll be pleasantly surprised by how tasty it is. Plus it's usually lower in fat, calories and cholesterol than most traditional pork and beef varieties.*

Apple Cider Turkey Breast

This Thanksgiving, rather than trying to heat all of your side dishes and the turkey in your oven (which can be a juggling act all by itself), why not cook your turkey in your air fryer? In this recipe, we infuse a boneless turkey breast with apple cider and coat it with lots of seasonings, so that every slice is extra-juicy and full of flavor. Did we mention the crispy skin? It makes this even more perfect.

Serves 6

Ingredients

1 tablespoon vegetable oil

¼ teaspoon paprika

¼ teaspoon onion powder

¼ teaspoon ground thyme

¼ teaspoon salt

¼ teaspoon black pepper

½ teaspoon chopped fresh parsley

1 (3-pound) boneless turkey breast

¾ cup apple cider or juice

Preparation

1 In a small bowl, combine oil, paprika, onion powder, thyme, salt, pepper, and parsley; mix well. Rub mixture evenly over turkey breast.

2 Preheat air fryer to 350 degrees F.

3 Coat air fryer basket with cooking spray. Place turkey skin-side up in basket and pour apple cider over it. Air-fry 10 minutes, turn over, and continue cooking 20 more minutes. Turn over one more time (now the turkey should be skin-side up) and cook an additional 5 to 7 minutes or until a meat thermometer (inserted in the thickest part) reaches 160 degrees F.

4 Remove turkey breast to a cutting board and let rest 5 to 10 minutes before slicing. (While it's resting, why not take a quick rest yourself? You've earned it!)

Test Kitchen Tip: *Spoon pan drippings over turkey for more of that delicious apple flavor.*

Marvelous Meat

Cilantro Lime Steak Fajitas

Fajitas are one of those dishes that everyone seems to like. (Maybe the smell and sizzle has something to do with it?) We feel these fajitas are best when you keep them pretty basic, since the skirt steak is amazing on its own. Of course, a few roasted peppers and onions doesn't hurt either. In the end, it's up to you whether or not to pile on the toppings. Either way, we're sure you're going to love these!

Makes 8

Ingredients

MARINADE

1 bunch fresh cilantro, stems removed (about 1 cup)

1-½ cups olive oil

2 tablespoons fresh lime juice

6 cloves garlic

1 teaspoon cumin

1 teaspoon salt

½ teaspoon black pepper

1 (2 to 2-½-pound) skirt steak, cut into 5-inch pieces

3 bell peppers, thinly sliced (1 green, 1 red, 1 yellow)

½ cup thinly sliced onion

1 tablespoon olive oil

½ teaspoon salt

¼ teaspoon black pepper

8 (4-inch) flour tortillas, warmed according to package directions

Preparation

1 In a food processor, combine Marinade ingredients and pulse until cilantro and garlic are coarsely chopped.

2 Place skirt steak in a resealable plastic bag along with marinade; toss to coat. Marinate for at least 2 hours in the refrigerator or overnight.

3 When you're ready to cook your fajitas, preheat air fryer to 400 degrees F. In a large bowl, combine bell peppers, onion, 1 tablespoon oil, ½ teaspoon salt, and ¼ teaspoon pepper; toss to coat evenly. Place bell pepper and onion mixture into air fryer basket and air-fry 12 to 15 minutes or until tender, shaking basket halfway through cooking. Remove to a bowl and cover to keep warm.

4 Remove steak from marinade; discard excess marinade. Place steak in basket, making sure not to overcrowd, and cook 7 to 9 minutes or until desired doneness, turning halfway through cooking. (We don't recommend cooking this cut of meat past medium or it'll start to get tough.)

5 Remove steak to a cutting board; let rest 5 minutes before slicing thinly across the grain. Place steak, peppers, and onions on flour tortillas and enjoy.

Asian Kitchen Beef & Broccoli

Typically, stir-frying veggies and beef means lots and lots of oil, but thanks to the air fryer, we no longer have to do that! This version of an Asian favorite is healthier and just as delicious. We think you'll especially love the homemade sauce; it brings everything together in the most perfect way. Serve this over some brown or white rice and dig in! (Whether or not to use chopsticks is totally up to you.)

Serves 4

Ingredients

1 (12-ounce) bag broccoli florets

½ onion, cut into half-moon slices

Cooking spray

2 tablespoons cornstarch

2 tablespoons all-purpose flour

½ teaspoon salt

½ teaspoon black pepper

1-¼ pounds thinly sliced top round steak, cut into ½-inch strips

ASIAN SAUCE

½ cup hoisin sauce

2 teaspoons sesame oil

2 tablespoons soy sauce

3 cloves garlic, minced

2 teaspoons minced fresh ginger

2 tablespoons water

Preparation

1 Preheat air fryer to 400 degrees F.

2 Coat air fryer basket with cooking spray. Place broccoli and onion in basket; lightly spray with cooking spray. Air-fry 4 minutes; shake basket and continue to cook 4 to 5 more minutes or until crisp-tender. Remove to a bowl; cover to keep warm.

3 In a large bowl, whisk cornstarch, flour, salt, and pepper. Add steak, in batches, and toss until evenly coated. Coat basket with cooking spray. Place half the steak strips in basket, arranging them so they aren't overcrowded; spray lightly with cooking spray and cook 2 minutes. Turn over, spray lightly with cooking spray, and continue to cook 2 to 3 more minutes or until no longer pink. Repeat with remaining steak strips.

4 Meanwhile, to make Asian Sauce, in a small saucepan over low heat, combine all ingredients.

5 In a large bowl, combine steak and veggies. Pour sauce over them; toss until evenly coated. Serve immediately.

Steak Skewers with Chimichurri Sauce

You would never think that steak skewers as tender and flavorful as these could have been cooked in an air fryer. But as you'll soon find out, it's the truth! This Argentinian-inspired dish is a real showstopper and so quick! In fact, after they've been given time to marinate, they're cooked in under 5 minutes. So on those days when you're craving tender and flavor-packed steak, make sure to come back to this recipe. We promise you won't be disappointed.

Serves 4

Ingredients

2 pounds boneless top sirloin steak, trimmed

CHIMICHURRI SAUCE

1-½ cups olive oil

2 tablespoons lemon juice

¾ cup fresh parsley, stems removed

8 cloves garlic

1 teaspoon salt

¼ teaspoon black pepper

½ teaspoon crushed red pepper

12 (4-inch) bamboo skewers, soaked in water for 15 minutes to prevent burning

Preparation

1 Cut steak into 12 strips, about ½-inch wide and 5-inches long (check out the photo for reference).

2 To make Chimichurri Sauce, in a food processor or in a blender, combine all sauce ingredients; process until it's pretty smooth. Reserve ½ cup of sauce until ready to serve.

3 Thread one strip of steak onto each skewer. Place in a 9- x 13-inch baking dish and pour sauce (minus what's been reserved) over steak. Cover and refrigerate for at least 2 hours or overnight.

4 Preheat air fryer to 400 degrees F. Coat air fryer basket with cooking spray. Put all skewers in basket (it's okay if they slightly overlap), discard extra sauce, and air-fry 4 minutes. Turn skewers and continue to cook 3 to 4 more minutes or until meat is cooked to desired doneness. Place on a serving platter and drizzle with reserved sauce.

Dressed Up Tenderloin with Roasted Mushrooms

This is definitely a special occasion recipe. What we discovered while testing this in our air fryer is that the hot air circulating around the meat not only sears it, but also allows to cook evenly. That means, the roast cooks perfectly from one end to the other. Once it's cooked, all that's left to do is spoon on some Béarnaise sauce and serve it with "roasted" mushrooms (also made in the air fryer!). This is a meal fit for royalty!

Serves 4

Ingredients

1-½ to 2 pounds beef tenderloin roast

1 teaspoon salt, divided

Coarse black pepper for sprinkling

8-ounces baby bella mushrooms, quartered

1 tablespoon vegetable oil

¼ teaspoon black pepper

1 (0.9-ounce) packet Béarnaise sauce mix, prepared according to package directions

Preparation

1 Preheat air fryer to 360 degrees F. Sprinkle beef with ½ teaspoon salt and the coarse black pepper. Coat air fryer basket with cooking spray. Put beef in basket and air-fry 8 minutes. Turn over and continue to cook 6 to 8 more minutes or until desired doneness. (If you like it medium-rare, the internal temperature that you should cook until is 135 degrees F.) Remove beef to a cutting board and let it rest about 10 minutes. (Beef will continue to cook while it's resting and should reach 145 degrees F.)

2 Meanwhile, in a medium bowl, toss mushrooms with oil, remaining ½ teaspoon salt, and the ¼ teaspoon black pepper. Place in basket and "roast" 3 to 4 minutes or until tender.

3 Slice beef, spoon the Béarnaise sauce over it, and serve with mushrooms.

Garlic & Herb Melt-Away Steak

Has this ever happened to you? You feel like grilling, but it's either raining, too hot, or you're out of propane or charcoal. On those days, why not turn to your air fryer? The fact that it can reach high temperatures means it locks in all the juicy flavors of the steak. To make things even better, we suggest finishing off your steaks with a homemade herbed butter that'll melt into all the nooks and crannies.

Serves 2

Ingredients

GARLIC HERB BUTTER

½ stick butter, softened

3 cloves garlic, minced

2 teaspoons chopped fresh parsley

1 teaspoon coarse black pepper

2 (8-ounce) strip steaks

Salt for sprinkling

Black pepper for sprinkling

Preparation

1 In a small bowl, combine butter, garlic, parsley, and coarse black pepper; mix well. Spoon butter mixture onto a piece of wax paper and form into a 1-inch log. Wrap tightly, so butter holds its shape; refrigerate 15 to 20 minutes or until butter firms up.

2 Preheat air fryer to 380 degrees F. Sprinkle both steaks with salt and pepper and place in air fryer basket. Air-fry 5 minutes. Turn over and continue to cook 2 to 3 more minutes for medium-rare or until desired doneness. (A meat thermometer should read at least 135 degrees F.)

3 Remove from basket, allow steaks to rest for a couple of minutes, then top each with 2 (¼-inch-thick) slices of herb butter. As it melts, the flavored butter will ensure that every bite is juicy and dripping with deliciousness.

Brown Sugar Bacon Meatloaf

Meatloaf is a favorite comfort food in households all over the country. In the Test Kitchen, we thought we'd made it every which way ... that is, until we realized we'd never made it in an air fryer. We quickly remedied that! As it turns out, meatloaf is easy to make in an air fryer. The meatloaf cooks evenly all over and the fat drips into the pan below. Extra comfort, less guilt!

Serves 4

Ingredients

1 pound ground beef

¼ cup finely chopped onion

½ cup Italian bread crumbs

1 egg

½ cup ketchup, divided

½ teaspoon salt

½ teaspoon black pepper

2 tablespoons water

2 tablespoons brown sugar

2 strips bacon

Preparation

1 Preheat air fryer to 350 degrees F.

2 In a large bowl, combine beef, onion, bread crumbs, egg, ¼ cup ketchup, the salt, and black pepper; mix well. Using your hands, form into an oval.

3 Make a 4-inch-wide foil sling (see page ix) and coat with cooking spray. Place meatloaf on sling and lower into air fryer basket. Add water to pan. (This will help prevent smoking.) Air-fry 15 minutes.

4 Meanwhile, in a small bowl, mix remaining ¼ cup ketchup and the brown sugar. Spread evenly over top of meatloaf, top with bacon, and continue to cook 12 to 15 more minutes or until meatloaf is no longer pink in center and bacon is crispy. Use foil sling to remove meatloaf from basket and allow to rest for 10 minutes before serving.

Outrageous Reuben Burgers

Outrageous burgers are really trendy these days. Not only does bigger seem to be better, but the more unusual they are, the more popular. To join in on the fun, we've created a deli-inspired burger that features everything we love about a Rueben in the form of a colossal burger. Just wait until you serve these ... their jaws are gonna drop in awe.

Makes 2

Ingredients

½ pound ground beef

¼ teaspoon garlic powder

¼ teaspoon salt

¼ teaspoon black pepper

½ cup coarsely chopped deli corned beef

1 (3-ounce) can sauerkraut, drained

4 slices Swiss cheese

¼ cup Russian dressing

4 slices rye bread

Preparation

1 Preheat air fryer to 370 degrees F.

2 In a large bowl, combine ground beef, garlic powder, salt, pepper, and corned beef (yup, the corned beef gets added to the ground meat); mix well. Form mixture into 2 equal-sized patties.

3 Coat air fryer basket with cooking spray, place patties in basket, and air-fry 5 minutes. Turn patties over and continue to cook 3 to 4 more minutes or until desired doneness. While patties are still in basket, top each with sauerkraut and 2 slices of cheese. Heat 1 minute or until cheese is melted.

4 Meanwhile, spread dressing evenly on 2 slices of bread. Place a burger on each and top with remaining bread. This is one HUGE sandwich so we definitely suggest cutting it in half before digging in.

Test Kitchen Tip: *Depending on how much fat the ground beef you're using has, you may find that the drippings start to smoke once they hit the pan. If so, add a couple of tablespoons of water to the pan, and voila, no more smoking.*

Mushroom Blue Cheese Burger Bowls

With so many of us watching our carbs (when we say watching, we mean not eating 'em), we knew we had to share a low carb burger recipe. That's why we came up with this bun-free recipe that turns your burger into a bowl. The whole idea behind a burger bowl is that you can then fill it with all of your favorite toppings – just like we did here. Who says carb eaters get to have all the fun?

Serves 2

Ingredients

1 pound ground beef

1 tablespoon steak sauce

½ teaspoon garlic powder

¼ teaspoon salt

¼ teaspoon black pepper

2 tablespoons butter

1 tablespoon vegetable oil

1-½ cups (4-ounces) sliced mushrooms

1 cup thinly sliced onion (half moons)

2 tablespoons crumbled blue cheese

Preparation

1 In a medium bowl, combine ground beef, steak sauce, garlic powder, salt, and pepper; mix well. Divide mixture in half and form into 2 oversized patties, each about 1-inch thick.

2 To form burger bowls, start by pressing a glass or 1-cup dry measuring cup into center of each patty. Remove glass (or cup) and, using your fingers, finish shaping meat to look like a bowl (see photo). The sides and bottom should be about ¼-inch thick.

3 Preheat air fryer to 350 degrees F. Using a foil sling (see page ix), lower one burger bowl into air fryer and air-fry 7 to 8 minutes or until cooked to desired doneness. Using foil sling, remove burger bowl from air fryer and repeat with second burger bowl.

4 Meanwhile, in a medium skillet over medium heat, heat butter and oil; sauté mushrooms and onion 5 to 7 minutes or until tender.

5 Fill each burger bowl with half of the sautéed mushrooms and onion and top with half of the crumbled blue cheese (the heat from the mushrooms will melt the cheese).

Summer's Best Stuffed Peppers

Every summer the Test Kitchen crew makes a trip to the farmer's market. On a recent trip we came back with baskets of tomatoes, peppers, and fudge (one of the vendors there makes the best walnut fudge ever, so we couldn't resist!). Then back in the Test Kitchen, while pigging-out on fudge, we whipped up these stuffed peppers in our air fryer. They were so good – it made the perfect end to a perfect day.

Makes 4

Ingredients

- ¾ pound ground beef
- ¾ cup cooked white rice
- 1 cup shredded mozzarella cheese, divided
- 1-½ cups spaghetti sauce, divided
- 1 teaspoon garlic powder
- ½ teaspoon salt
- ¼ teaspoon black pepper
- 4 medium bell peppers, tops removed, and seeded (see Tip)

Preparation

1 In a medium skillet over medium heat, cook ground beef until no pink remains, stirring occasionally to break up; drain.

2 In a large bowl, combine beef, rice, ½ cup cheese, ½ cup spaghetti sauce, the garlic powder, salt, and pepper; mix well.

3 Preheat air fryer to 330 degrees F. Line bottom of air fryer basket with aluminum foil (to keep peppers from sliding around). Place ½ cup water in air fryer pan. Stuff each pepper with an equal amount of beef mixture and place in basket. Air-fry 18 to 20 minutes or until peppers are tender. Top peppers evenly with remaining ½ cup cheese and continue to cook 1 to 2 minutes or until cheese is melted.

4 Meanwhile, in a small saucepan over low heat, heat remaining 1 cup spaghetti sauce. Spoon sauce over peppers and serve.

Test Kitchen Tip: *Make this as colorful as you like by mixing and matching the colors of the peppers. And, so that the peppers don't tip over, trim a bit off the bottom so that they sit flat in the basket.*

Beer-Infused Cheese Dogs

Do you remember going to Lum's restaurants? If so, then you might recall that they were known for cooking their hotdogs in beer. Even though the chain is just a distant memory, there's no reason why we can't relive those tasty times. So whether you're looking to bring back those fond memories or want to experience their hotdogs for the first time, there's no better time than right now to give these a try.

Serves 4

Ingredients

1 (12-ounce) package hot dogs (4 large)

½ cup beer

½ cup shredded cheddar cheese

4 hot dog rolls (we used New England-style)

Pickled banana peppers, drained, for garnish

Pickle relish, drained, for garnish

Preparation

1 Preheat air fryer to 380 degrees F. Cut 3 slits in each hot dog. (This will prevent them from splitting while they cook.) Pour beer into air fryer pan and place hot dogs in air fryer basket. Air-fry 4 to 5 minutes or until heated through, turning halfway through cooking.

2 Meanwhile, sprinkle cheese evenly in each roll. (Yup, the cheese goes on the roll before we put the hot dog in it.) Place hot dogs in rolls and place back in basket, in batches if necessary. Cook 30 seconds or until cheese is melted and buns are warmed. Garnish with banana peppers and relish; serve.

Rosemary Lemon Roasted Pork

Here's a perfect example of why we love "roasting" meat in the air fryer. Not only is our pork seared to perfection on the outside, but it's juicy as can be on the inside. By circulating hot air around the roast, the air fryer helps seal in all of the natural juices. It also helps that our roast cooks at a low temperature. (Some things just taste better when they're cooked at lower temperatures.) Every bite of this flavorful pork is mouthwatering.

Serves 6

Ingredients

2 tablespoons olive oil

3 cloves garlic, minced

1 sprig fresh rosemary, coarsely chopped

1 lemon cut in half, divided

½ teaspoon salt

½ teaspoon coarse black pepper

1 (2-pound) boneless pork loin

Preparation

1 Preheat air fryer to 310 degrees F.

2 In a large bowl, combine oil, garlic, rosemary, zest and juice from ½ the lemon, salt, and pepper; mix well. Place pork in bowl and coat evenly with rosemary lemon mixture.

3 Cut remaining ½ lemon into quarters. Place pork in air fryer basket and place lemon quarters around it. Air-fry 10 minutes, turn pork over, and continue to cook 15 more minutes. Turn roast over one more time and continue to cook 10 to 15 more minutes, or until a meat thermometer inserted in center reaches 135 degrees F. (Make sure not to overcook pork or it will be dry.)

4 Remove pork from basket and let rest on a cutting board 10 minutes. As it rests, the temperature will continue to rise to about 145 degrees for a perfect medium doneness. Slice and serve.

Hand-Breaded Buttermilk Pork Chops

This is a spin-off of a recipe that we got from an Amish friend of ours. Obviously, the big difference is that she didn't cook her chops in an electric air fryer, but we bet that if she tried our version, she'd be impressed. What makes these so good is their simplicity. And when you team up the chops with our homemade applesauce, they're a hands-down winner.

Serves 2

Ingredients

2 shoulder pork chops (about 1-inch thick)

Salt for sprinkling

Black pepper for sprinkling

½ cup all-purpose flour

1 teaspoon onion powder

1 teaspoon garlic powder

½ cup buttermilk

Cooking spray

Serving Suggestion: *To make our homemade applesauce, bring ¾ cup water and ½ cup sugar to a boil in a soup pot. Add 6 large Granny Smith apples that you've peeled, cored, and cut into thin slices. Stir in ¼ teaspoon cinnamon, and ¼ teaspoon nutmeg. Then simmer, covered, for 25 to 30 minutes or until apples are tender, making sure to stir occasionally to break up the apples. This makes a lot, so you'll probably have plenty left over to serve with another meal.*

Preparation

1 Sprinkle pork chops evenly with salt and pepper. Place flour, onion powder, and garlic powder in a shallow dish; mix well. Pour buttermilk into a second shallow dish. With your hands, dip chops in buttermilk one at a time, (shake gently to remove excess buttermilk), then in flour mixture, turning to coat both sides. Then dip chops back into buttermilk (gently shake off excess again) and finish by dredging them in flour mixture. Preheat air fryer to 360 degrees F.

3 Coat air fryer basket with cooking spray. Place chops in basket in batches,if necessary. Lightly coat tops with cooking spray, and air-fry 15 minutes. Turn chops over and continue to cook 4 more minutes or until desired doneness (a minimum of 145 degrees F). Serve chops with applesauce. (See Serving Suggestion.)

Pork Roast Marsala

Did the pork throw you off? We know, you're probably used to seeing veal or chicken Marsala, but we think you're going to love this one too. As a matter of fact, now that we've made it a bunch of times, we like our air fryer "roasted" pork much better. In this recipe, the sauce doesn't smother the meat, but rather complements it. When you serve this for dinner, you'll be on the receiving end of compliments too!

Serves 5

Ingredients

3 tablespoons butter, softened

2 teaspoons chopped fresh parsley

1 teaspoon onion powder

½ teaspoon salt

½ teaspoon black pepper

2 to 2-½ pounds boneless pork loin roast

MARSALA SAUCE

3 tablespoons butter

¼ cup finely chopped onion

8 ounces fresh mushrooms, sliced

½ cup Marsala wine

½ teaspoon garlic powder

¼ teaspoon salt

⅛ teaspoon black pepper

½ cup chicken broth

1 tablespoon all-purpose flour

Preparation

1 Preheat air fryer to 330 degrees F.

2 In a small bowl, combine 3 tablespoons butter, the parsley, onion powder, ½ teaspoon salt, and ½ teaspoon black pepper; mix well. Rub herb butter evenly over all sides of pork loin.

3 Coat air fryer basket with cooking spray. Place pork in basket and air-fry 10 minutes. Turn pork over and continue to cook 10 more minutes. Repeat this process twice, turning every 10 minutes, for a total of 40 minutes, or until a meat thermometer reaches 140 degrees F. Remove from basket, place roast on a cutting board, and let rest.

4 Meanwhile to make Marsala Sauce, in a large skillet over medium heat, melt 3 tablespoons butter; sauté onion and mushrooms 5 minutes or until softened. Add wine, garlic powder, ¼ teaspoon salt, and ⅛ teaspoon pepper; heat until mixture is hot, stirring occasionally. In a small bowl, whisk broth and flour until smooth. Stir into skillet and heat until sauce thickens.

5 Carve pork into ½-inch slices and serve with sauce.

Triple Crunch Pork Chops

If you're looking at the list of ingredients and thinking, "What the heck?!" we don't blame you. We agree, it is a bit odd. However, you gotta trust us on this one. Ya see the combination of the slightly sweetened cereal, mixed with the nuts and butter crackers is truly remarkable and gives these chops a really satisfying crunch. Not to mention that they're super juicy and tender too. Give it a try; it'll all make sense!

Serves 4

Ingredients

¾ cup finely crushed Cap'n Crunch® cereal

¼ cup finely crushed butter-flavored crackers

¼ cup finely chopped pistachio nuts

4 (¾-inch-thick) boneless pork chops

Salt for sprinkling

Black pepper for sprinkling

Cooking spray

Preparation

1 Preheat air fryer to 330 degrees F.

2 In a shallow dish, combine cereal, crackers, and nuts; mix well.

3 Sprinkle pork chops evenly with salt and pepper. Coat both sides of chops with cooking spray, then dip in cereal mixture, pressing firmly to ensure all sides are coated evenly and that breading won't blow off in the air fryer.

4 Coat air fryer basket with cooking spray. Place chops in basket, lightly coat tops with cooking spray, and air-fry 7 minutes. (You may need to cook these in batches.) Turn chops over, give them another spray and continue to cook 7 to 9 more minutes or until no longer pink in center (145 degrees F) and breading is golden.

Country Stuffed Pork Tenderloin

Pork tenderloin is one of the best values in the meat case. It's the filet mignon of pork, only smaller, which makes it perfect for cooking in an air fryer. This is one of those recipes that's weeknight-friendly (it cooks up so quickly!), but worth saving for a special occasion. Just like filet mignon, it's super tender and can be stuffed for even more goodness.

Serves 3

Ingredients

1 pork tenderloin (about 1-pound)

2 tablespoons olive oil

2 cloves garlic, minced

¾ teaspoon dried thyme, divided

¼ teaspoon onion powder

½ teaspoon salt

¼ teaspoon black pepper

1 (6-ounce) package pork stuffing mix, prepared according to package directions

½ cup dried cranberries

1 (12-ounce) jar pork gravy

Preparation

1 Place pork on a cutting board and cut into 3 equal pieces. (Each piece should be about 3-½ inches long.) Using a sharp knife, cut a pocket lengthwise down top of each piece of pork, being careful not to cut all the way through.

2 In a small bowl, combine oil, garlic, ½ teaspoon thyme, the onion powder, salt, and pepper; mix well. Rub mixture over pork. In a medium bowl, combine stuffing with cranberries; mix well. Spoon about ½ cup of stuffing into the slit in each piece of pork, gently pressing into each pocket. (Be generous!) Preheat air fryer to 330 degrees F.

3 Coat air fryer basket with cooking spray. Place stuffed pork into basket and air-fry 12 to 14 minutes or until pork is at least medium (145 degrees F) or to desired doneness. Let rest 5 minutes before serving.

4 Meanwhile, in a small saucepan over medium heat, combine pork gravy and remaining ¼ teaspoon dried thyme; heat thoroughly. Serve warmed gravy with pork and enjoy.

Test Kitchen Tip: *If you have some stuffing that won't fit into the pork, heat that separately in the microwave and serve it on the side.*

Maple-Dijon Country-Style Ribs

Before we go any further, let us introduce you to country-style ribs. Like spare ribs and baby backs, these are a cut of their own. They're meatier, leaner and mostly boneless, which makes them really versatile and perfect for feeding the heartiest of eaters. We slathered ours with a maple-Dijon glaze, that's happy dance-worthy. And if you prefer a glaze that's a bit more caramelized, give them an extra minute – it's no problem!

Serves 4

Ingredients

½ cup real maple syrup

3 tablespoons Dijon mustard

2 teaspoons Worcestershire sauce

3 pounds country-style pork ribs

Onion powder for sprinkling

Salt for sprinkling

Black pepper for sprinkling

Preparation

1 Preheat air fryer to 360 degrees F.

2 In a small bowl, combine maple syrup, Dijon mustard, and Worcestershire sauce; mix well and set aside.

3 Sprinkle ribs on both sides with onion powder, salt, and pepper. Coat air fryer basket with cooking spray. Working in batches, if necessary, place ribs in basket in a crisscross fashion. (This way the air can easily circulate around them, so they cook evenly.) Air-fry 8 minutes, turn ribs over, and bring the ones in the bottom of the pile to the top; continue to cook 6 more minutes.

4 Generously brush ribs with half the maple-Dijon mixture and cook 5 minutes. Turn ribs over again. Brush with remaining mixture and continue to cook 5 to 7 more minutes or until ribs are no longer pink inside and sauce begins to caramelize.

Test Kitchen Tip: *Yes there's lots of turning going on in this recipe, but that's what ensures that they brown perfectly and that each bite is packed with flavor.*

Sticky Finger Spareribs

Whether you serve these at a backyard bash, game day party, or just because, get ready to have a messy-good time. (Did the name give it away?) With all the bone-suckin', finger-lickin', and lip-smackin' you're going to be doing, it's important to make sure you've got plenty of napkins on hand. And for those of you who don't like getting your fingers messy, it's time to flip the page.

Serves 3

Ingredients

1 (2-½ to 3-pound) rack pork spareribs, cut into 3 sections

¼ cup vegetable oil

¼ cup soy sauce

1 tablespoon molasses

2 tablespoons packed brown sugar

1 teaspoon ground ginger

1 teaspoon dry mustard

1 teaspoon garlic powder

1 teaspoon salt

½ teaspoon black pepper

Preparation

1 Place spareribs in a large pot and add just enough water to cover. Over medium-high heat, boil ribs 35 to 40 minutes or until fork-tender; drain well. Let cool slightly, then cut into individual ribs, between each bone.

2 Meanwhile, in a large bowl, combine remaining ingredients; mix well. Place ribs in sauce and toss until evenly coated. Pour remaining sauce into a small bowl and set aside. Preheat air fryer to 390 degrees F.

3 Coat air fryer basket with cooking spray. Place ribs in basket in a crisscross fashion (this way the air can easily circulate around them, so they cook evenly). Air-fry 5 minutes, then brush with more sauce. Turn ribs over and brush with remaining sauce. Continue to cook 4 to 5 more minutes or until sauce begins to caramelize.

Greek-Style Rack of Lamb with Mint Jelly

If cooking lamb has always intimidated you, then you have to try this one. It couldn't be easier. All you need to do is rub, air-fry ("roast"), and enjoy. When you're done, you'll end up with moist and meaty lamb chops, flavored with Greek-style seasonings and finished off with a bit of mint jelly. By the way, these are just as good served as an appetizer as they are a fancy-shmancy main course.

Serves 6

Ingredients

2 tablespoons olive oil

3 cloves garlic, minced

1 teaspoon dried oregano

¾ teaspoon salt

¼ teaspoon black pepper

2 racks of lamb (about 2-½ pounds)

½ cup mint jelly

Preparation

1 Preheat air fryer to 380 degrees F.

2 In a small bowl, combine oil, garlic, oregano, salt, and pepper; mix well. Rub mixture evenly over lamb. Coat air fryer basket with cooking spray and place one or both of the racks in basket. (You may need to cook them in batches depending on the size of your air fryer; just make sure you don't overcrowd them.)

3 Air-fry lamb 5 minutes, turn racks over, and continue to cook 3 more minutes. Turn racks over one more time and continue to cook 4 to 6 more minutes or until a meat thermometer registers at least 145 degrees F, or until desired doneness.

4 Meanwhile, in a small saucepan over low heat, heat jelly until warmed. Carve ribs between the bones and serve with mint jelly.

Test Kitchen Tip: *Yes we've said it before, but we wanted to remind you again that if your air fryer starts to smoke due to the drippings, a couple tablespoons of water in the pan should do the trick.*

Sensational Seafood, Pasta, and More

Lightning-Fast Shrimp Tacos

Are your taste buds ready for this? We sure hope so, because these shrimp tacos deliver a ton of flavor! Not only do we season the shrimp with a kicked-up blend of spices, but we also make our own Sassy Lime Slaw to take these up a notch. Sure your local taco shop might have some great tacos, but you can make even better ones at home ... and they'll be done lightning fast.

Serves 4

Ingredients

¼ cup all-purpose flour

2 teaspoons chili powder

1 teaspoon ground cumin

⅛ teaspoon cayenne pepper

½ teaspoon salt

12 ounces small raw shrimp, peeled, tails removed (thawed if frozen)

Cooking spray

8 (6-inch) flour tortillas, warmed

SASSY LIME SLAW

3 cups shredded coleslaw

2 tablespoons rice vinegar

2 tablespoons vegetable oil

1 tablespoon lime juice

½ teaspoon salt

Preparation

1 Preheat air fryer to 400 degrees F. In a large bowl, mix flour, chili powder, cumin, cayenne pepper, and salt. Place shrimp on a paper towel-lined plate and pat dry. Add shrimp to spice blend and toss until evenly coated.

2 Coat air fryer basket with cooking spray. Working in batches, place shrimp in basket, making sure not to overcrowd, and air-fry 4 minutes. Turn shrimp over and lightly spray with cooking spray. Continue to cook 3 to 4 more minutes or until firm. Repeat with remaining shrimp.

3 In another large bowl, combine all ingredients for Sassy Lime Slaw; toss until evenly coated.

4 Place slaw evenly down center of tortillas, then top with shrimp. Serve immediately.

Southern Cornbread Stuffed Shrimp

There's no question that cooking in an air fryer saves time (so much so, you might even be able to pick up a new hobby!). These for example, only take four minutes to cook after you stuff 'em. Yes, FOUR minutes! And when you bite into these butter-basted shrimp with a cornbread and bacon stuffing, get ready for a real Southern treat. A glass of sweet tea and you're all set.

Serves 4

Ingredients

7 strips cooked bacon, crumbled (see Tip)

3 tablespoons finely chopped celery

2 corn muffins, crumbled

2 tablespoons mayonnaise

1 pound colossal (13-15 count) raw shrimp, peeled, with tails on (thawed if frozen)

2 tablespoons butter, melted

1 teaspoon seafood seasoning (we used Old Bay®)

Preparation

1 Preheat air fryer to 400 degrees F.

2 In a medium bowl, combine bacon, celery, muffin crumbles, and mayonnaise; mix well and set aside.

3 Butterfly shrimp by cutting lengthwise along the outer curve, ¾ of the way through. Open the slit and devein. In a medium bowl, combine butter and seafood seasoning. Add shrimp and toss until evenly coated. Mound a tablespoon or so of the corn muffin mixture into each slit and using your finger, gently pack in the filling, stuffing the shrimp.

4 Coat air fryer basket with cooking spray. Working in batches, place stuffed shrimp in basket and air-fry 4 minutes or until shrimp turn pink. Repeat with remaining shrimp. Serve immediately.

Test Kitchen Tip: *Bacon is easy to cook in the air fryer. All you have to do is place 1/4 cup water in air fryer pan. Working in batches, place bacon in air fryer basket, being careful not to overcrowd or overlap. Air-fry 5 minutes at 390 degrees F. Turn bacon over and continue to cook 4 to 5 more minutes or until desired crispness. Repeat with remaining bacon. Drain on paper towels, and crumble, if desired.*

Peachy Mango Tropical Shrimp

Typically, when we make fried shrimp, the kitchen ends up smelling like a local fish fry. (And if you're like one of us, you've been known to leave the pot of oil sitting on the stove to deal with the next day.) You won't have to worry about either of those things with this recipe! Air-frying the shrimp means no funky fried food odors, plus the basket and pan go right into the dishwasher for easy clean up. Go ahead, throw on a tropical shirt and celebrate!

Serves 3

Ingredients

¾ cup peach-mango preserves

2 tablespoons orange juice

¾ cup all-purpose flour

½ teaspoon salt

½ teaspoon cayenne pepper

2 eggs

¼ cup coconut milk
(not cream of coconut)

12 ounces extra-large shrimp, peeled and deveined, with tails left on (thawed if frozen)

Cooking spray

Preparation

1 In a small bowl, combine preserves and orange juice; mix well and set aside. (This will be the sauce that gives the shrimp a fresh, tropical taste.)

2 In a shallow dish, combine flour, salt, and cayenne pepper; mix well. In another shallow dish, whisk eggs and coconut milk until well combined.

3 Preheat air fryer to 400 degrees F. Dredge shrimp in flour mixture, then egg mixture, then back in flour mixture, coating completely. Coat air fryer basket with cooking spray. Working in batches, place shrimp in basket, making sure not to overcrowd. Generously spray shrimp with cooking spray. Air-fry 3 minutes, turn over, and generously spray once more with cooking spray. Continue to cook 3 to 4 more minutes or until golden. Repeat with remaining shrimp.

4 Place the first batch back in the basket and cook 1 minute to warm up. Spoon sauce over shrimp and serve immediately.

Pesto Scallops
with Toasted Walnuts

To say that you'll go nuts for these is an understatement (pun intended). The scallops are melt-in-your-mouth tender, the pesto sauce adds a fresh and welcoming taste, and the roasted nuts over the top add a subtle crunch. And to think that these can be done, from start to finish, in under 15 minutes. Everything about this recipe is remarkable!

Serves 4

Ingredients

⅓ cup walnuts halves

1 cup lightly packed fresh basil leaves

½ cup plus 1 tablespoon olive oil, divided

½ cup grated Parmesan cheese

1 clove garlic

¼ teaspoon salt

½ teaspoon paprika

½ teaspoon sea salt

¼ teaspoon coarse black pepper

1 pound sea scallops, patted dry

Preparation

1 Preheat air fryer to 390 degrees F. Place walnuts in air fryer basket and air-fry 2 minutes or until toasted. Shake basket after 1 minute, so that they toast evenly. Allow to cool slightly, then coarsely chop. Place 1 tablespoon of chopped nuts aside. (You'll use them later.) Place remaining nuts in a food processor.

2 To prepare the pesto, add basil, ½ cup olive oil, the Parmesan cheese, garlic, and salt to nuts in food processor; process until smooth. (If you prefer, you can use a blender for this step.)

3 In a medium bowl, combine remaining 1 tablespoon olive oil, the paprika, sea salt, and pepper; mix well. Add scallops and toss gently until evenly coated. Place scallops in basket. Cook 4 minutes, turn over, and continue to cook 3 to 4 more minutes or until scallops are firm.

4 Serve scallops on a bed of pesto and sprinkle with remaining chopped walnuts.

Maryland-Style Crab Cakes

If you like Maryland-style crab cakes, then you're going to love these! They're the real deal, as good as it gets, or as some might still say, the "cat's pajamas." What makes them so good is that they're packed with lump crabmeat, rather than lots of filler. Cooking them in the air fryer makes them perfect, never greasy, and super moist.

Makes 4

Ingredients

½ cup mayonnaise

1 egg

1 tablespoon Dijon mustard

2 cloves garlic, minced

2 teaspoons seafood seasoning (we used Old Bay®)

¼ teaspoon salt

¼ teaspoon black pepper

¾ cup bread crumbs

1 pound lump crabmeat

Cooking spray

Preparation

1 Preheat air fryer to 400 degrees F.

2 In a large bowl, whisk together mayonnaise, egg, mustard, garlic, seafood seasoning, salt, and pepper. Gently stir in bread crumbs and crabmeat until just combined. (Do not overmix.) Form mixture into 4 crab cakes and place on a platter.

3 Coat air fryer basket with cooking spray. Working in batches, if necessary, place crab cakes in basket. Lightly spray each crab cake with cooking spray.

4 Air-fry 5 minutes, turn crab cakes over, and continue to cook 5 to 6 more minutes or until heated through and golden brown. Repeat with remaining crab cakes.

Poached Salmon with Dill Sauce

Did you know that you can not only "fry" in your air fryer, but that you can also broil, bake, braise and even poach in it? So don't let the name fool ya! If you didn't already love all that your air fryer can do, you will now. As a bonus, it makes clean-up a breeze and keeps your kitchen cool! Now put it to work and enjoy some light and healthy salmon with a refreshing dill sauce.

Serves 4

Ingredients

1 (1-½-pound) salmon fillet

½ lemon, cut into thin slices

¼ cup dry white wine

DILL SAUCE

¼ cup mayonnaise

¼ cup sour cream

2 teaspoons chopped fresh dill

¼ teaspoon salt

⅛ teaspoon black pepper

Preparation

1. Preheat air fryer to 350 degrees F. Place a 12-inch piece of aluminum foil on a work surface. Place salmon in center of foil and bring up sides of foil slightly.

2. Place lemon slices on top of salmon and pour wine over top. Bring edges of foil together, then fold to seal. (Make sure foil packet is tightly sealed to allow steaming, but not too tight, as we want there to be room around the fish.) Place foil packet in air fryer basket and air-fry 15 to 16 minutes or until fish flakes easily with a fork. (Be careful when opening up the foil packet, as it will be very hot.)

3. Meanwhile, to make Dill Sauce, combine all ingredients in a small bowl; mix well and keep refrigerated until ready to serve.

4. Carefully unwrap fish and remove lemon slices. Serve immediately or refrigerate and serve chilled with Dill Sauce.

Fresh Salmon Croquettes with Asian Ginger Sauce

Do you have any memories of eating salmon croquettes as a child? Believe it or not, this is an old-time favorite. While your grandma might've made hers with canned salmon, we like to use fresh salmon when we can. We also added an Asian flair. With a slight kick from the wasabi and a deliciously creamy ginger sauce, these croquettes are unforgettably tasty.

Makes 4

Ingredients

1 pound skinless salmon fillets, cut into chunks

2 slices fresh white bread, torn up

2 scallions, sliced

1 tablespoon lemon juice

½ teaspoon salt

¼ teaspoon black pepper

Cooking spray

ASIAN GINGER SAUCE

½ cup mayonnaise

½ teaspoon ground ginger

1 teaspoon soy sauce

2 tablespoons dried wasabi peas, coarsely chopped

Preparation

1 Preheat air fryer to 370 degrees F. In a food processor, place salmon, bread, scallions, lemon juice, salt, and pepper; pulse until coarsely chopped and well combined. Form mixture into 4 oval croquettes.

2 Coat air fryer basket with cooking spray. Working in batches, if necessary, place croquettes in basket. Spray with cooking spray. Air-fry 5 minutes, turn over, and continue to cook 3 more minutes or until cooked through. Repeat with remaining croquettes.

3 Meanwhile, to make Asian Ginger Sauce, in a small bowl, combine all sauce ingredients and mix well.

4 Serve warm, topped with chopped wasabi peas, and Asian Ginger Sauce on the side.

Five Star
Fish Fillets

This is the kind of dish you'd probably expect to find on the menu of a five star restaurant, but surprise … we've made it into a quick weeknight meal! While we did use imitation crabmeat (to keep things budget-friendly), you'll still feel like a million bucks when you serve this. And hey, if you want to splurge a little bit, you can use real crab! Either way, these fish fillets are five star-worthy.

Makes 4

Ingredients

8 ounces imitation crabmeat, flaked

½ cup finely crushed saltine crackers

¼ cup finely chopped celery

3 tablespoons mayonnaise

½ teaspoon garlic powder

½ teaspoon black pepper

4 (6-ounce) flounder fillets or other white-fleshed fish fillets

2 tablespoons butter, melted, divided

½ lemon for juicing

Preparation

1 Preheat air fryer to 380 degrees F.

2 In a medium bowl, combine crabmeat, cracker crumbs, celery, mayonnaise, garlic powder, and pepper; mix well.

3 Place fish fillets on a 4-inch-wide foil sling (see page ix). Brush fillets with 1 tablespoon melted butter and drizzle with lemon juice. Spoon crabmeat mixture evenly over each fillet. Drizzle with remaining butter. Place in air fryer basket in batches, if necessary.

4 Air-fry 6 to 8 minutes or until fish flakes easily with a fork. Repeat with remaining fillets. Serve immediately.

Good for You: *Our body loves when we eat colorful veggies. So rather than buying white potatoes, try the colorful varieties along with lots of green veggies.*

Great Greek Fish Packets

When you start out with a mild-tasting white fish like tilapia, it's only right that you pair it with bold flavors. That's why we went Greek with this one! From the tanginess of the lemon and feta to the fruity-saltiness of the Kalamata olives, this fish is anything but bland. Plus it cooks in a foil packet (just like our salmon on page 172!), so you know it's going to be easy.

Makes 2

Ingredients

2 cups fresh spinach

2 (6-ounce) tilapia fillets

½ teaspoon dried oregano

Salt for sprinkling

Black pepper for sprinkling

2 teaspoons lemon juice

¼ cup crumbled feta cheese

2 tablespoons sliced, pitted Kalamata olives

1 tablespoon chopped roasted red peppers (optional)

2 teaspoons olive oil

Preparation

1 Preheat air fryer to 380 degrees F. Place 2 (12- x 18-inch) pieces of aluminum foil on a work surface.

2 Evenly divide spinach on each piece of foil. Place a tilapia fillet on top of spinach. Sprinkle each evenly with oregano, salt, and pepper. Drizzle with lemon juice. Evenly sprinkle with cheese, olives, and roasted red peppers, if desired. Drizzle with oil. Bring edges of foil together, then fold to seal. (Make sure foil packet is tightly sealed, but not too tight, as we want there to be room around the fish.)

3 Place foil packets in air fryer basket and air-fry 12 to 13 minutes or until fish flakes easily with a fork. (Be careful when you open up foil packets as they will be steaming hot.)

Test Kitchen Tip: *This recipe, like many other recipes in this book that are designed for 2 people, can be easily increased to feed 4 or 6 simply by doubling or tripling the recipes. However, you may have to cook it in batches, depending on the size of your air fryer.*

"New" England Fish Fillets

This recipe is inspired by a favorite from across the pond. In England, a dish of fish and chips (their word for french fries) is traditionally served on newspaper and enjoyed with malt vinegar, so we thought it'd be fun to do the same. As you can see, we got a little creative with the breading (it's made with potato flakes!) and served ours with homemade potato chips (recipe on page 212). It's quite tasty!

Makes 4

Ingredients

1-½ pounds cod or haddock, cut into 4 pieces

Salt for sprinkling

Black pepper for sprinkling

½ cup yellow cornmeal

½ cup instant potato flakes

1 teaspoon onion powder

½ stick butter, melted

Cooking spray

Preparation

1 Preheat air fryer to 350 degrees F. Sprinkle fish evenly with salt and pepper.

2 In a shallow dish, combine cornmeal, potato flakes, and onion powder. Place melted butter in another shallow dish. Dip fish in melted butter, then cornmeal mixture, pressing coating firmly onto fish.

3 Coat air fryer basket with cooking spray. Working in batches, place fish in basket and lightly coat each fillet with cooking spray.

4 Air-fry 6 to 7 minutes or until thinner pieces flake easily with a fork. Remove thinner pieces and continue cooking thicker pieces 4 to 5 more minutes or until those fillets also flake easily with a fork.

Down South Blackened Catfish

We love catfish in the Test Kitchen, especially the US farm-raised variety. It's fresh-tasting, meaty, and mild, which means there are lots of tasty ways to prepare and serve it. In this case, we used a homemade blackened seasoning mix. It's flavorful, without being so hot you can't taste the fish. Pair your blackened catfish with some hush puppies and sautéed greens, and you've got yourself a Southern-style meal.

Makes 4

Ingredients

- 2 teaspoons paprika
- 1 teaspoon crushed dried thyme
- ½ teaspoon onion powder
- ½ teaspoon garlic powder
- ½ teaspoon salt
- ½ teaspoon sugar
- ¼ teaspoon cayenne pepper
- ¼ teaspoon black pepper
- 4 (6-ounce) farm-raised catfish fillets

Preparation

1 Preheat air fryer to 380 degrees F.

2 In a small bowl, combine paprika, thyme, onion powder, garlic powder, salt, sugar, cayenne pepper, and black pepper; mix well. Sprinkle catfish evenly with seasoning mixture on both sides, pressing into fish with your fingers.

3 Coat air-fryer basket with cooking spray. Working in batches, if necessary, place fish in basket. Air-fry 7 to 9 minutes or until fish flakes easily with a fork.

Butter-Bathed Lobster Tails

Oh yeah, it's time to get fancy with your air fryer! Did you know that the air fryer's unique design makes cooking lobster so easy? That's because air fryers can steam and "broil" at the same time. Pretty cool, right? If you don't happen to have any lobster in your freezer right now, it might be time to order some online (maybe from QVC?) or from your local fish counter. These buttery tails are a must-try!

Makes 2

Ingredients

2 (8-ounce) lobster tails (thawed, if frozen)

¼ cup water

1 lemon, cut into quarters

2 tablespoons butter, melted

Preparation

1 With a pair of kitchen shears, cut top of lobster shells down the middle and gently split open. Loosen meat in shell and gently lift so that it lays on top of the cut shell (see photo). Make sure to leave base of tail attached. (Fan out lobster tail so it looks picture-perfect.)

2 Preheat air fryer to 370 degrees F. Pour water into air fryer pan and squeeze the juice from half the lemon quarters into pan.

3 Brush lobster tails with melted butter and squeeze juice from remaining lemon quarters over tails. Place tails and lemon quarters (the ones you squeezed over the tails) into air fryer basket. Air-fry 7 to 9 minutes or until lobster meat turns white all the way through.

Serving Suggestion: *To give these a bit more color, sprinkle them with some paprika before serving. And if you like lots of butter for dunking like we do, melt some extra, so you can dip away.*

Kelly's Roasted Shrimp & Linguine

Kelly, from our Test Kitchen, loves shrimp and is crazy about pasta. (She is Italian, after all!) So when she challenged the rest of us to come up with an easy shrimp and pasta dinner, we couldn't disappoint her. While we didn't make the pasta in our air fryer, we did manage to make the yummiest garlicky roasted shrimp ever in it. Yes, it's Kelly approved!

Serves 3

Ingredients

8 ounces linguine

1 stick butter

8 cloves garlic, minced

12 ounces extra-large raw shrimp, peeled, with tails left on (thawed if frozen)

¼ cup dry white wine

¾ teaspoon salt

¼ teaspoon black pepper

1 tablespoon lemon juice

1 tablespoon chopped fresh parsley

Preparation

1 Cook linguine according to package directions; set aside.

2 Meanwhile, in a large skillet over medium-low heat, melt butter. Stir in garlic and heat 1 minute (do not brown); remove from heat. Place shrimp in a large bowl and add 1 tablespoon of the garlic-butter; toss until evenly coated.

3 Preheat air fryer to 400 degrees F.

4 Pour wine into air fryer pan and place shrimp in basket. (Overlapping is fine.) Air-fry 3 minutes, then stir shrimp to ensure they cook evenly. Continue to cook 2 to 3 more minutes or until shrimp are pink and cooked through.

5 Meanwhile, add salt, pepper, lemon juice, and parsley to the remaining garlic-butter in skillet; mix well. Reduce heat to low and warm 2 minutes. Add linguine to garlic-butter and toss until evenly coated. Heat an additional 3 minutes or until hot. Serve linguine topped with the shrimp.

Good Ole
Spaghetti & Meatballs

Do you remember the TV commercials that proclaimed that Wednesday is "Spaghetti Day"? Honestly, we think any day that ends in a "y" works too. (Who's going to turn away a bowl of piping hot spaghetti with homemade meatballs on say ... a Thursday?!) After testing and tasting many versions, we love the way these meatballs cook in our air fryer. If ya want, ya could simmer the meatballs in some sauce before serving, but that's up to you.

Serves 4

Ingredients

- 1 pound spaghetti
- ½ pound ground pork
- ½ pound ground beef
- ¾ cup Italian bread crumbs
- ⅓ cup grated Parmesan cheese
- ½ cup water (at room temperature)
- ¼ cup chopped fresh parsley
- 1 egg
- 1-½ teaspoons garlic powder
- ½ teaspoon salt
- ½ teaspoon black pepper
- 1 (24-ounce) jar spaghetti sauce

Preparation

1 Cook spaghetti according to package directions; set aside.

2 Meanwhile, in a large bowl, gently combine all ingredients except sauce and spaghetti. (Be careful not to overmix, as meatballs will get tough.) Form into 8 (2-inch) meatballs. Preheat air fryer to 360 degrees F.

3 Coat air fryer basket with cooking spray. Place meatballs in basket. Air-fry 6 minutes, turn over, and continue to cook 6 to 7 more minutes or until no longer pink in center.

4 Warm sauce, spoon over pasta, and top with meatballs.

So Many Options: *To change these up, feel free to experiment with different kinds of shredded cheese or topping blends.*

Cracker-Crusted Mac 'n' Cheese

We like to think we know a little more than most when it comes to making really good mac 'n' cheese. After all, over the years, we've made dozens of variations of this family favorite. Our air fryer version certainly doesn't disappoint. It's extra cheesy, ooey gooey, and topped with a yummy, buttery cracker crust. Basically, it's got everything a good mac 'n' cheese needs to make everyone smile!

Serves 4

Ingredients

1-½ cups elbow macaroni

½ stick butter, divided

2 tablespoons all-purpose flour

½ teaspoon dry mustard

½ teaspoon salt

¼ teaspoon black pepper

1-¼ cups milk

1-½ cups shredded sharp cheddar cheese

½ cup diced mozzarella cheese

¼ cup coarsely crushed butter crackers

Preparation

1 Cook macaroni according to package directions; set aside.

2 Meanwhile, in a medium saucepan over medium heat, melt 3 tablespoons butter. Add flour, dry mustard, salt, and pepper; cook 1 minute. Gradually stir in milk, bring to a boil, and cook until thickened, stirring constantly. Add cheddar cheese and continue stirring until melted. Add macaroni and mozzarella cheese to the cheese sauce; mix well.

3 Spoon mixture into a 6-inch deep-dish metal pan. (Many air fryers come with a pan like this, but if yours didn't you can use a 1.5-quart baking dish or disposable pan that'll fit into your air fryer basket.)

4 Preheat air fryer to 330 degrees F. Place pan in air fryer basket and air-fry 12 minutes.

5 Meanwhile, melt remaining 1 tablespoon butter in microwave. Stir in cracker crumbs and mix until evenly coated. Sprinkle cracker mixture over macaroni and continue to cook 3 to 5 more minutes or until heated through and topping is golden.

Roasted Veggies with Penne

Don't you just hate it when the veggies in your pasta dish are watery and wimpy? We sure do! That's why we prefer roasting our veggies (in the air fryer, of course!) before adding them to the penne. Roasted veggies have more texture and flavor, which makes them extra tasty. This recipe is a game changer – you'll see!

Serves 4

Ingredients

8 ounces penne pasta

2 tablespoons olive oil

1 teaspoon garlic powder

1 teaspoon salt

½ teaspoon black pepper

1 zucchini, cut into 1-inch chunks

1 red bell pepper, cut into 1-inch chunks

8 ounces fresh mushrooms, cut into quarters

1 cup grape tomatoes, cut in half

½ onion, cut into 1-inch chunks

2 tablespoons butter

1 cup vegetable or chicken broth

¼ cup crumbled goat cheese

2 tablespoons slivered fresh basil

Preparation

1 Cook pasta according to package directions; set aside.

2 Meanwhile, in a large bowl, combine olive oil, garlic powder, salt, and black pepper; mix well. Add zucchini, bell pepper, mushrooms, tomatoes, and onion; toss until evenly coated. Preheat air fryer to 400 degrees F.

3 Place veggies in air fryer basket. Air-fry 5 minutes. Shake basket to mix veggies and continue cooking 4 to 5 more minutes or until tender.

4 In a large skillet over medium heat, melt butter; add broth and bring to a boil. Add pasta and cook 3 to 4 minutes or until heated through.

5 Place pasta mixture in a large bowl, add veggies, goat cheese, and basil; toss to coat. Serve immediately.

Three Cheese Spaghetti Bake

We've already introduced you to Good Ole Spaghetti & Meatballs (page 188), now it's time for something a little more non-traditional. Just take a look at the photo on the opposite page! Have you ever made anything like it? If you have, betcha' it wasn't in your air fryer! Impress your family by serving up a SLICE of spaghetti for dinner. They're going to love it.

Serves 4

Ingredients

- 8-ounces spaghetti
- 2 eggs
- ½ cup ricotta cheese
- ¼ cup grated Parmesan cheese
- ½ teaspoon garlic powder
- ¼ teaspoon salt
- 1 cup spaghetti sauce, divided
- ½ cup shredded mozzarella cheese

Serving Suggestion: If you like things saucy, feel free to ladle some extra sauce on each slice.

Preparation

1 Cook spaghetti according to package directions. Preheat air fryer to 320 degrees F.

2 Meanwhile, coat a 6-inch pan with cooking spray. [Many air fryers come with a pan like this. If not, you can pick one up at a local store that carries kitchen products.]

3 In a large bowl, whisk eggs. Add ricotta and Parmesan cheeses, garlic powder, salt, and ½ cup spaghetti sauce; mix well. Add spaghetti and toss until evenly coated. Spoon evenly into pan and top with ¼ cup spaghetti sauce.

4 Place pan in air fryer basket and air-fry 20 minutes or until set in center. Spoon remaining ¼ cup spaghetti sauce on top and sprinkle with mozzarella cheese. Turn off air fryer and place basket back inside; let it sit 2 to 3 minutes or until cheese is melted.

5 Remove pan from air fryer and let sit 10 minutes to cool slightly. Invert pan onto a plate, then flip back over so the cheese is on top. Cut into wedges and serve.

Antipasto Stuffed Portabella Mushrooms

These are no run-of-the-mill stuffed mushrooms. These mushrooms are colossal-sized and stuffed with our favorite antipasto ingredients. And just in case you were wondering ... yes, these are definitely filling. Drizzle on some olive oil and a bit of balsamic vinegar and dive right in! (If you're feeling really fancy, get yourself some crusty bread and a glass of Chianti you deserve it.)

Makes 4

Ingredients

- 4 (3-inch) portabella mushrooms
- ½ cup diced deli salami (from about a ½-inch-thick slice)
- 1-½ cups fresh spinach leaves, coarsely chopped
- 2 tablespoons chopped roasted red peppers
- 1 cup shredded mozzarella cheese
- ⅓ cup Italian bread crumbs
- 2 cloves garlic, minced
- ¼ teaspoon salt
- ¼ teaspoon black pepper
- 2 tablespoons olive oil

Preparation

1 Preheat air fryer to 330 degrees F.

2 Gently clean mushrooms by wiping them with damp paper towels. Remove stems; set aside caps. Coarsely chop stems.

3 In a large bowl, combine chopped mushroom stems, salami, spinach, roasted red peppers, mozzarella cheese, bread crumbs, garlic, salt, black pepper, and oil; mix well. Evenly fill each mushroom cap with mixture.

4 Coat air fryer basket with cooking spray. Place stuffed mushrooms in basket. Air-fry 8 to 10 minutes or until heated through and mushroom caps are tender.

So Many Options: *To change these up, feel free to experiment with different kinds of shredded cheese or topping blends. Maybe add some pitted olives, pepperocini, or more of your favorite Italian deli meats. (Just make sure you cut them into small pieces.)*

Mediterranean Falafel Delights

Falafel may be a popular food in the Middle East, but we decided to give ours a Mediterranean flair. When you serve them, we suggest putting out a platter with warm pita bread, diced tomatoes, cucumbers, and some tzatziki sauce. That way, everyone can build their own falafel pita sandwich! Who says you need a passport to take your taste buds on a food-venture?

Makes 18

Ingredients

1 (15.5-ounce) can chickpeas, rinsed and drained, with ¼ cup liquid reserved

1 cup plain bread crumbs

2 eggs

2 tablespoons chopped fresh parsley

1 teaspoon lemon juice

1 teaspoon garlic powder

½ teaspoon salt

½ teaspoon black pepper

1 teaspoon ground cumin

Cooking spray

Preparation

1 Preheat air fryer to 400 degrees F. Line a baking sheet with wax paper and lightly coat with cooking spray.

2 In a food processor, combine all ingredients (including reserved liquid), except cooking spray. Process on medium-high speed until mixture is smooth and well blended. (Mixture should be similar in consistency to peanut butter.)

3 Using your hands (wet them to prevent the mixture from sticking), shape mixture into 18 (1-½ inch) balls and flatten slightly (see photo). Place on baking sheet. Working in batches, if necessary, add falafel to air fryer basket, being careful not to overcrowd. Air-fry 5 minutes; turn over and continue to cook 1 to 2 more minutes or until outside is crisp. Repeat with remaining falafel.

Serving Suggestion: *You can either pick up tzatziki from the store, or make your own by combining a couple of large cucumbers (that have been peeled, seeded, and grated) with 2 cups of sour cream, a couple of teaspoons of lemon juice, a 1/4 cup of chopped fresh dill, and a bit of salt and pepper. It's so fresh and tasty!*

Mile-High Eggplant Caprese Towers

This is the kind of recipe that really demonstrates just how good an air fryer can fry. Before you could only make something like this in a deep-fryer or by pan-frying it in lots of oil. Now, all you need to do is bread the eggplant like you would normally, and just air-fry it. You save yourself a greasy mess and a whole lot of extra calories! (Also, isn't this tower impressive?)

Makes 6

Ingredients

1 cup Italian bread crumbs

¼ cup all-purpose flour

2 eggs

1 large eggplant, cut into 12 slices

Cooking spray

2 large tomatoes, each cut into 6 slices

1 (16-ounce) fresh mozzarella ball, cut into 12 slices

Olive oil for drizzling

6 sprigs fresh basil

Coarse black pepper for sprinkling

Preparation

1 Preheat air fryer to 400 degrees F. In a shallow dish, place bread crumbs. In another shallow dish, place flour. Whisk eggs in a third shallow dish. Dip eggplant slices in flour, then egg, then bread crumbs, coating completely.

2 Coat air fryer basket with cooking spray. Working in batches, place eggplant in basket in a single layer. Air-fry 4 minutes, turn slices over, and spray lightly with cooking spray. Continue to cook 3 to 4 more minutes or until tender and breading is golden. Repeat with remaining eggplant.

3 To build the towers, place one slice of eggplant on a plate. Top with a tomato slice and a mozzarella slice, another slice of eggplant, another mozzarella slice, and finally another tomato slice (see photo). Repeat with remaining eggplant, mozzarella, and tomato slices to build 5 more towers.

4 Drizzle eggplant towers with oil. Garnish each with a sprig of basil and some freshly ground black pepper.

Quinoa & Bean Patties

This is the recipe that might just convince you to give Meatless Mondays a try. These patties are hearty enough to fill you up (no matter how hungry you are!) and full of nutrient-rich ingredients. Not only are these tasty, but you get lots of protein, fiber, vitamins, and minerals, too. Delicious and nutritious!

Makes 4

Ingredients

¼ cup quinoa

¾ cup water

1 (15-ounce) can black beans, rinsed and drained

½ cup bread crumbs

¼ cup diced yellow or red bell pepper

2 tablespoons minced onion

2 cloves garlic, minced

2 teaspoons ground cumin

½ teaspoon salt

1 egg, beaten

Preparation

1 In a saucepan over high heat, bring quinoa and water to a boil; reduce heat to low. Stir, cover, and simmer 15 to 20 minutes, or until quinoa is tender and water has been absorbed.

2 In a medium bowl, roughly mash black beans with a fork until you have a paste-like mixture, leaving some whole beans.

3 Preheat air fryer to 390 degrees F.

4 In a large bowl, combine quinoa, bread crumbs, bell pepper, onion, garlic, cumin, salt, and egg; mix well. Add black beans and using your hands, mix well. Form mixture into 4 burger-shaped patties.

5 Coat air fryer basket with cooking spray. Working in batches, place patties in basket and air-fry 5 minutes. Turn patties over and continue to cook 5 to 6 more minutes or until heated through and patties develop a crisp crust. Repeat with remaining patties. After the second batch is done, place first batch back in for 1 minute to warm up.

Great
Go Alongs

Kicked-Up Poutine

Poutine is said to have originated in Canada, in the 1950s. Over the years, it's become pretty popular, and has made its way down south to many parts of the U.S. We think it's pretty darn tasty (fries, cheese curds, and gravy - yes, please!), so we decided to put our own spin on it. Here you've got all the basics, plus we kick it up by adding some some yummy onion rings. This is the kind of side dish you sit back and relax with.

Serves 4

Ingredients

8 ounces frozen crinkle-cut French fries

Cooking spray

8 ounces frozen breaded onion rings

½ cup cheddar cheese curds

½ cup beef gravy, warmed

Preparation

1 Preheat air fryer to 400 degrees F.

2 Coat air fryer basket with cooking spray. Place fries in basket and spray with cooking spray. Air-fry 7 minutes, then shake basket.

3 Place onion rings on top of fries and lightly coat with cooking spray. Continue to cook 7 more minutes or until crispy.

4 Place fries and onion rings on a serving platter. Top with cheese curds and pour gravy over the top. Serve immediately.

Good for You: *Do you realize how much fat, calories and cholesterol you cut by air frying your fries and onion rings rather than deep frying them? Now, we can indulge in them every now and then without all the guilt.*

Loaded Curly Fry Nachos

It's amazing how many different ways there are to cut a potato. In this book alone we have more than a dozen ways to change up the look of America's favorite veggie. When you combine the whimsical, twirly cut of curly fries with your favorite nacho toppings, you end up with a "nacho-everyday" super side dish.

Serves 4

Ingredients

½ (26-ounce) bag frozen curly fries

½ cup shredded Mexican cheese blend

½ cup diced tomato

1 scallion, sliced

¼ cup sliced black olives

1 fresh jalapeño, sliced

Sour cream for garnish (optional)

Preparation

1 Preheat air fryer to 400 degrees F.

2 Coat air fryer basket with cooking spray. Place curly fries in basket. Air-fry 5 minutes, shake basket, and continue to cook 5 to 6 more minutes or until fries are crispy and golden.

3 Place hot fries on a platter and top with cheese, tomato, scallion, olives, and jalapeño. Dollop with sour cream, if desired, and serve with plenty of napkins.

So Many Options: *As with all our recipes, feel free to change this up by adding any of your nacho favorites. Remember, there are no rules when it comes to mixing and matching toppings.*

Salt & Vinegar Waffle Fries

We know this is a popular flavor combo on potato chips, so we decided to shake things up (pardon the pun!) by trying it on our waffle-cut fries. One bite and we knew we had a winner! We love how crispy these get after air frying them, and the vinegar adds a kick without making them soggy. These are so good, it's hard to believe they didn't come out of a vat of hot oil!

Serves 5

Ingredients

1 (22-ounce) package frozen waffle fries

Cooking spray

2 tablespoons white vinegar

¾ teaspoon salt

Preparation

1 Preheat air fryer to 400 degrees F.

2 Coat air fryer basket with cooking spray. Add half the fries to basket and spray with cooking spray. Air-fry 5 minutes, then shake basket so they cook evenly. Continue to cook 5 to 6 more minutes or until crispy. Place fries in a large bowl and set aside. Repeat with remaining fries.

3 When the second batch of fries is cooked, add the first batch back into basket for 1 minute to warm up. Place in a large bowl, drizzle with vinegar, and sprinkle with salt; toss until evenly coated. Serve immediately.

Homemade Potato Chips

Okay, let's be honest, these are a lot more work than simply opening up a bag of chips; however, they're also a lot better tasting and a lot healthier. Plus can you imagine the look on the faces of your family and friends when you tell them that you made your own potato chips? They'll think you're nuts ... at least until they try their first bite. Then they'll realize you're brilliant!

Serves 4

Ingredients

2 medium russet baking potatoes

1 teaspoon vegetable oil

½ teaspoon salt, divided

Preparation

1 Cut potatoes into extra-thin slices, using either a very sharp knife or a mandoline slicer. (You want the slices no more than ⅛-inch thick.)

2 In a medium bowl of ice water, soak potato slices 15 minutes. (This will help them crisp up while they cook.) Preheat air fryer to 350 degrees F.

3 Drain water and spread out potatoes on paper towels, patting them dry. Return potatoes to bowl. Add oil and ¼ teaspoon salt; toss to coat evenly.

4 Working in two batches, place half the potato slices in air fryer basket. Air-fry 5 minutes, turn slices over, and continue to cook 5 more minutes. Turn slices over one more time and continue to cook 5 to 7 minutes or until crispy and golden. (Turning these frequently is so important, so no slacking off or your chips will stick together.) Repeat with remaining slices.

5 Empty basket into a large serving bowl, sprinkle with remaining ¼ teaspoon salt, and serve.

Parmesan-Crusted Potato Wedges

Potato wedges are kind of like "baked potato meets french fry." They're crispy on the outside, but so tender on the inside. We like that we can eat them with our fingers, but they're hearty enough to be the main go-along on our plate (although enjoying 'em with a side of colorful veggies doesn't hurt!). And they're really flavorful, especially since they're dipped in butter before they're coated in garlic-Parmesan.

Serves 4

Ingredients

½ cup plain bread crumbs

½ cup grated Parmesan cheese

½ teaspoon garlic powder

½ teaspoon salt

¼ teaspoon black pepper

6 tablespoons butter, melted

2 large baking potatoes, unpeeled

Preparation

1 In a shallow dish, combine bread crumbs, Parmesan cheese, garlic powder, salt, and pepper; mix well and set aside. In another shallow dish place melted butter.

2 Preheat air fryer to 400 degrees F.

3 Cut potatoes lengthwise into quarters; then cut each quarter lengthwise into thirds. Dip each wedge in melted butter, then into bread crumb mixture, coating completely.

4 Working in batches, if necessary, place breaded potato wedges in air fryer basket, overlapping one layer in a crisscross pattern. Air-fry 5 minutes, turn over, and continue to cook 5 to 6 more minutes or until potatoes are tender and coating is crispy. Repeat as needed with remaining wedges. When all the batches are done, you can pile all the wedges up in the basket and rewarm them for 1 minute or so before serving.

Really Good French Fries

When it came to naming this recipe, we could have given it some fancy name, but we felt that after tasting these (or shall we say chowing down on a platter of them) we should call them what they are – Really Good French Fries. They're not greasy, just perfectly crisp and tasty. And when you serve these with our Dilly Dill-icious Ketchup, they're REALLY really good!

Serves 4

Ingredients

4 medium baking potatoes

2 cups ice cubes

2 tablespoons vegetable oil

½ teaspoon salt, divided

DILLY DILL-ICIOUS KETCHUP

½ cup ketchup

2 teaspoons dill pickle juice

Preparation

1   Peel potatoes. (If you want you can leave the skins on; that's up to you.) Cut potatoes lengthwise into ¼-inch-thick slices. Then cut each slice into ¼-inch fries. Place cut potatoes in a large bowl and cover with cold water. Add ice and let sit 30 minutes. (The ice water will help the potatoes crisp up during cooking.) Drain potatoes and place on paper towels; pat dry with additional paper towels.

2   Preheat air fryer to 400 degrees F. In a large bowl, toss potatoes with oil until evenly coated. Place potatoes in air fryer basket and air-fry 10 minutes. Sprinkle with ¼ teaspoon salt and continue to cook 10 to 12 minutes or until golden brown and tender, shaking basket halfway through cooking.

3   Meanwhile, in a small bowl, make Dilly Dill-icious Ketchup by combining ketchup and pickle juice; mix well. Set aside.

4   Place fries on a platter, sprinkle with remaining ¼ teaspoon salt, and serve with Dilly Dill-icious ketchup.

Glazed Sweet Potato Steak Fries

If you had a blah kind of day and feel like you could make it better with something comforting on your plate, then these are just what the doctor ordered. We aren't quite sure what makes these so comforting, but we've noticed they have what it takes to turn "blah" into "ahh." It could be the cinnamon in the coating or the extra sweetness of the sweet potato (and the maple butter glaze!). Try 'em and see if you can pinpoint what it is!

Serves 4

Ingredients

2 large sweet potatoes

2 tablespoons vegetable oil

½ teaspoon ground cinnamon

½ cup maple syrup

1 tablespoon butter

Sea salt for sprinkling

Preparation

1　Preheat air fryer to 400 degrees F.

2　Peel potatoes and cut into quarters lengthwise, then cut each quarter into thirds. In a large bowl, combine potatoes, oil, and cinnamon; toss to coat completely.

3　Place a single layer of potatoes in air fryer basket, then place a second layer in basket in the opposite direction. Air-fry 7 minutes, turn potatoes over, and continue to cook 7 more minutes or until tender.

4　Meanwhile, in a small microwave-safe bowl, combine syrup and butter. Heat in microwave 45 to 60 seconds or until butter is melted; stir to combine.

5　Remove potatoes to a serving dish, sprinkle with sea salt, and drizzle with maple glaze.

Dijon Roasted Red Skin Potatoes

If these potatoes could talk, they'd probably say, "Try me! Try me!" but maybe in a French accent, since they're inspired by French-style potatoes. It's hard not to love them — the Dijon-butter coating is so addictive! Whether you serve these as a side with chicken or steak, you can't go wrong. Bon appétit!

Serves 4

Ingredients

1 pound small red skin potatoes, quartered

2 cloves garlic, minced

2 teaspoons vegetable oil

⅓ cup Dijon mustard

½ stick butter, melted

1 tablespoon chopped fresh parsley

Preparation

1 Preheat air fryer to 400 degrees F.

2 In a medium bowl, combine potatoes, garlic, and oil; toss until evenly coated. Place potatoes in air fryer basket and air-fry 5 minutes.

3 Meanwhile, in a medium bowl, whisk mustard and butter; toss with hot potatoes.

4 Return potatoes to basket and cook an additional 4 minutes. Shake basket to toss potatoes and continue to cook 4 more minutes or until potatoes are tender and crispy. Sprinkle with parsley before serving.

Caesar-Style Potato Salad

No we're not kidding you, we made potato salad in our air fryer and we loved it! What sets this apart from your standard potato salad is our air-fried, "roasted" potatoes. They have a richer and nuttier flavor. And when you toss them in a light Caesar vinaigrette, along with a few crunchy veggies, it's just perfect. You can serve this one warm or chilled; either way is just scrumptious!

Serves 4

Ingredients

1-½ pounds red skin potatoes, cut into ½-inch chunks

⅓ cup plus 1 tablespoon Caesar vinaigrette dressing, divided (see Tip)

¼ cup chopped celery

¼ cup chopped red bell pepper

4 strips bacon, cooked and crumbled

Shaved Parmesan cheese for garnish

Preparation

1 Preheat air fryer to 400 degrees F.

2 In a large bowl, toss potatoes with 1 tablespoon Caesar dressing until evenly coated. Place potatoes in air fryer basket and air-fry 7 minutes. Stir potatoes and continue to cook 7 to 8 more minutes or until fork-tender. Place potatoes in a bowl and let cool slightly.

3 Add celery, bell pepper, bacon, and remaining ⅓ cup Caesar dressing; toss until evenly coated. Garnish with Parmesan cheese and serve.

Test Kitchen Tip: *When you're at the market looking at all the salad dressings, we suggest you pick up a bottle of Caesar dressing that's more oil and vinegar-based than a creamy one that looks like ranch dressing.*

Twice-Baked Loaded Potatoes

Warning – these are likely to make you never want a plain ole baked potato ever again. We'd say we're sorry, but we're not. The reason these are so great is that we stuff all of the good stuff (your favorite baked potato toppings) into an already baked potato, before baking it again. Simply put, every bite is packed with the flavors you love. This one deserves a double YUM!

Makes 4

Ingredients

4 medium russet baking potatoes

Cooking spray

¼ cup sour cream

2 tablespoons butter, melted

¼ cup shredded cheddar cheese

½ teaspoon salt

¼ teaspoon black pepper

Bacon bits for garnish

Scallion slices for garnish

Preparation

1 Preheat air fryer to 380 degrees F. Pierce each potato several times with a fork. Coat potatoes with cooking spray and place in air fryer basket.

2 Air-fry 35 to 38 minutes or until fork-tender; let cool slightly. (This range may vary depending on how big or small your potatoes are.)

3 Slice about ½-inch off top of each potato and scoop out pulp, leaving about a ¼-inch-thick potato shell; place pulp in a medium bowl. Add sour cream, butter, cheese, salt, and pepper to bowl; mix well. Spoon mixture evenly into potato shells.

4 Preheat air fryer to 350 degrees F. (This shouldn't take long since you just baked the potatoes.) Place stuffed potatoes in basket. Cook 8 to 10 minutes or until potatoes are heated through and tops get a bit golden. Top with bacon and scallions and serve immediately.

Old World Pierogi

It's easy to make pierogi exactly how you like them in your air fryer (no matter what they are stuffed with). If you like them plump and buttery, adding water to the pan does the trick, as the steam will do just that. However, if you prefer your pierogi a bit crispier, a spritz of oil will crisp these up, no problem.

Serves 4

Ingredients

⅓ cup water

1 (16-ounce) package frozen potato pierogi

2 tablespoons butter

¼ teaspoon salt

⅛ teaspoon black pepper

Sour cream for garnish

Chopped fresh chives for garnish

Preparation

1 Preheat air fryer to 320 degrees F.

2 Place water in air fryer pan. (The water will plump up the pierogi as they cook.) Place pierogi in air fryer basket. Air-fry 4 minutes, turn, and continue to cook 5 to 6 more minutes or until heated through. (If you like your pierogi crispier, you can spray them with a bit of oil at this point and let them cook for another minute or so.)

3 In a medium microwave-safe bowl, melt butter in microwave. Add salt, pepper, and pierogi; toss until evenly coated. Serve immediately topped with sour cream and chives.

So Many Options: *If you've never tried frozen pierogi, you're in for a real treat. They come with all sorts of fillings ... everything from a simple seasoned potato, to potato mixed with farmer cheese, cheddar, bacon, or even sauerkraut.*

Toasted Marshmallow Sweet Potato Rounds

We've baked 'em, mashed 'em, and smashed 'em, and even turned them into biscuits. Now thanks to our air fryer and a very creative Test Kitchen team (if we do say so ourselves), we've come up with a new way to turn these sweet spuds into a melt-in-your-mouth go-along that's toasty delicious. (We'll leave it up to you to decide who gets the most marshmallows on top!)

Serves 4

Ingredients

2 large sweet potatoes, unpeeled

2 tablespoons vegetable oil

½ teaspoon salt

¼ cup light brown sugar

2 tablespoons butter, melted

1 cup mini marshmallows

Preparation

1 Preheat air fryer to 390 degrees F.

2 Place sweet potatoes on a cutting board and trim off each end. Cut potatoes into 1-inch-thick slices.

3 In a large bowl, combine oil and salt; mix well. Add potato slices and toss until evenly coated. Working in batches, if necessary, place slices in air fryer basket in a single layer, and air-fry 6 minutes. Turn over and continue to cook 7 more minutes or until fork-tender. Remove to a platter and repeat with remaining slices as needed.

4 To finish these off, again working in batches if necessary, return slices to basket in a single layer. Sprinkle each slice with 1 teaspoon brown sugar. Drizzle melted butter evenly over brown sugar and arrange marshmallows on each slice. Cook 1 to 2 minutes or until marshmallows are lightly toasted. Repeat with remaining slices as needed. Serve immediately.

Crispy Sesame Artichoke Hearts

Don't go flipping the page because you think this recipe sounds too complicated or fancy. As a matter of fact, it couldn't get any easier! The recipe starts with canned artichokes, so you don't even have to know how to trim or cut an artichoke. It's simply drain, bread, and air-fry. These may be simple, but the taste is anything but.

Serves 4

Ingredients

½ cup panko bread crumbs

2 teaspoons sesame seeds

½ teaspoon garlic powder

½ teaspoon onion powder

½ teaspoon salt

¼ teaspoon black pepper

1 egg

¼ cup all-purpose flour

1 (14-ounce) can quartered artichoke hearts, drained well and patted dry

Cooking spray

Preparation

1 In a shallow dish, combine bread crumbs, sesame seeds, garlic powder, onion powder, salt, and pepper; mix well. In a second shallow dish, whisk egg. Place flour in another shallow dish.

2 Preheat air fryer to 400 degrees F. Dip each artichoke heart in flour, then in egg, then in bread crumb mixture, pressing firmly to coat. Spray air fryer basket with cooking spray. Working in batches, if necessary, place artichoke hearts in basket and lightly spray with cooking spray. Don't overcrowd.

3 Air-fry 3 minutes, turn artichoke hearts over, and continue to cook 3 more minutes or until golden.

Lemon-Parmesan Krispy Kale

Before you get started, we want to let you know that this is not a recipe for dehydrated kale chips. These are more of a hybrid between the best sautéed spinach you've ever eaten and crispy roasted kale. Our kale is fresh-tasting (not bitter) and light, which means you can probably get the whole family to eat it! The lemon drizzle and grated Parmesan cheese add a perfect finishing touch.

Serves 4

Ingredients

1 (12-ounce) bunch kale

2 tablespoons olive oil

½ teaspoon garlic powder

¼ teaspoon salt

¼ teaspoon black pepper

2 teaspoons lemon juice

1 tablespoon grated Parmesan cheese

Preparation

1 Preheat air fryer to 400 degrees F.

2 Wash kale and pat dry with paper towels. Remove and discard stems. Cut leaves into 3-inch pieces.

3 In a large bowl, combine oil, garlic powder, salt, and pepper; mix well. Add kale and toss until evenly coated.

4 Working in two batches, place half the kale in air fryer basket and air-fry 3 to 4 minutes or until edges begin to get crispy. Repeat with remaining kale.

5 Place kale in a large bowl, drizzle with lemon juice, and toss gently. Sprinkle with Parmesan cheese and serve immediately.

Honey-Orange Glazed Carrots

Did you know that roasting veggies helps bring out their natural sweetness? There's a reaction that happens when you cook them without water, which causes the sugars in the veggies to break down and caramelize. Pretty neat, huh? Now you can use your air fryer to do the same thing! To make these carrots even sweeter, we top them with a citrus-infused honey glaze. This simple side dish pairs perfectly with just about anything.

Serves 4

Ingredients

2 tablespoons butter

2 teaspoons brown sugar

2 tablespoons honey

1 teaspoon orange zest

1 [16-ounce] bag baby carrots

1 teaspoon vegetable oil

½ teaspoon salt

⅛ teaspoon black pepper

Preparation

1 Preheat air fryer to 380 degrees F.

2 In a small saucepan over low heat, combine butter, brown sugar, honey, and orange zest. Heat until hot, stirring occasionally.

3 In a medium bowl, toss carrots with oil, salt, and pepper and place in air fryer basket. Air-fry 7 minutes. Shake basket to mix carrots and continue to cook 6 to 7 more minutes or until tender.

4 Place carrots in a large bowl; drizzle with honey-orange mixture and toss until evenly coated.

Mexican-Style Corn on the Cob

Corn on the cob is a summertime favorite, especially when it's slathered with lots of butter! But this year, we wanted to try something new, so we did some research to find other ways that people are enjoying it. What we found was this Mexican-style version, popular with street vendors in the Southwest. It's still got the butter, but with a little kick to it. Plus, there's cheese and lime to make it extra tasty.

Makes 5

Ingredients

6 tablespoons butter, melted

1-½ teaspoons chili powder

2 tablespoons chopped fresh cilantro

5 ears of fresh corn, husks removed

¼ cup grated Cotija cheese (see Tip)

1 lime, cut into wedges

Preparation

1 In a small saucepan over low heat, melt butter with chili powder and cilantro; mix well.

2 Preheat air fryer to 380 degrees F. Brush corn evenly with butter mixture. Place corn in air fryer basket (it's okay for the corn to overlap a bit) and air-fry 8 to 10 minutes, turning halfway through cooking.

3 Remove corn from basket, sprinkle with cheese, and squeeze wedges of fresh lime over corn. Serve immediately.

Test Kitchen Tip: *Cotija cheese is a dry, Mexican grating cheese that's on the saltier side. If you can't find it among the other cheeses in your supermarket, you can substitute with Parmesan or feta.*

Italian Stuffed Zucchini Boats

You won't need an oar to enjoy these boats! Instead we suggest you bring a healthy appetite and a fork. We felt we had to include this recipe in the book since every time we've made them, we've gotten loads of comments on how great they are. If you're new to these, you're in for a real treat; these are going to be your new air fryer favorite. Be prepared for a "boat-load" of compliments!

Makes 4

Ingredients

2 small zucchini, sliced in half lengthwise

1 tablespoon olive oil

2 tablespoons finely chopped onion

¾ cup diced tomato

¼ cup Italian-flavored bread crumbs

1 tablespoon grated Parmesan cheese

½ teaspoon garlic powder

¼ teaspoon salt

⅛ teaspoon black pepper

½ cup water

¼ cup shredded mozzarella cheese

Preparation

1 Preheat air fryer to 360 degrees F.

2 With a spoon, scoop meat out of zucchini halves, leaving a ¼-inch wall all around; set aside shells and finely chop the scooped-out zucchini.

3 In a medium skillet over medium heat, heat oil until hot. Sauté chopped zucchini, onion, and tomato 2 minutes or until tender. Remove from heat. Stir in bread crumbs, Parmesan cheese, garlic powder, salt, and pepper until well mixed. Spoon mixture evenly into zucchini shells and place in air fryer basket.

4 Pour water into air fryer pan. Air-fry 10 to 12 minutes or until zucchini shells are tender. Sprinkle with mozzarella cheese and continue to cook 1 minute or until cheese is melted. .

Bacon-Wrapped Asparagus Bundles

One of the best ways to cook perfectly crispy bacon is in the air fryer. Coincidentally, an air fryer is also the perfect appliance for roasting veggies. (Find out why on page 234.) So, of course, we had to bring the two together. This may be our simplest go-along recipe ever, but it's absolutely fabulous. Plus it goes with just about anything ... like a juicy grilled steak!

Makes 4

Ingredients

16 spears fresh asparagus, trimmed to 6 inches

4 slices thick-cut bacon

Black pepper for sprinkling

Preparation

1 Preheat air fryer to 400 degrees F.

2 Wrap 4 asparagus spears with a slice of bacon, leaving both ends unwrapped (see photo); place in air fryer basket and repeat with remaining asparagus spears and bacon. Sprinkle bundles with pepper.

3 Air-fry 9 to 10 minutes or until bacon is crisp and asparagus is crisp-tender. Serve piping hot.

Crispy Onion Petals

We're crying tears of joy (and maybe the onion has something to do with it...) because now we can enjoy one of our favorite restaurant appetizers at home. Instead of "frying" the onion whole, we decided to go with these bite-sized petals. They're easier to make and eat. Plus since our version gets cooked in the air fryer, they're a lot healthier too.

Serves 4

Ingredients

1 large yellow onion

2 tablespoons all-purpose flour

½ cup buttermilk

1 cup plain bread crumbs

1 teaspoon garlic powder

1 teaspoon paprika

⅛ teaspoon cayenne pepper

1 teaspoon salt

Cooking spray

Serving Suggestion: *The best part of these is dipping or drizzling them with your favorite sauce. Some of our favorites are ranch and Russian dressing.*

Preparation

1 Peel onion and cut in half. Cut each half into 1-inch sections and separate onion layers. Put onion in a medium bowl along with flour; toss until evenly coated.

2 Pour buttermilk into a shallow dish. In another shallow dish, combine bread crumbs, garlic powder, paprika, cayenne pepper, and salt; mix well.

3 Preheat air fryer to 400 degrees F. One piece at a time, quickly dip floured onion pieces into buttermilk, shaking off excess, then into bread crumb mixture. Press firmly so that the coating sticks, and place pieces in air fryer basket. (It's okay for the pieces to overlap, but you may need to work in batches so that all the pieces cook evenly.) Generously spray onion pieces with cooking spray.

4 Air-fry 4 minutes, turn pieces over, spray again, and continue to cook 3 to 4 more minutes or until crispy and golden brown.

Simple & Sweet Plantains

Have you ever seen a plantain? They're a Caribbean favorite that look like oversized bananas and can vary in color, from green to almost black. Unlike bananas, plantains need to be cooked before eaten. How you cook 'em depends on what stage of ripening they're at. For instance, in this recipe you'll want to use plantains that are brown or almost black, as these are sweetest and most tender.

Serves 4

Ingredients

2 very ripe plantains

2 tablespoons vegetable oil

¼ teaspoon salt

Preparation

1 Preheat air fryer to 400 degrees F.

2 Peel plantains and place on a cutting board. Cut plantains at an angle into ½-inch-thick slices.

3 In a medium bowl, combine plantain slices, oil, and salt; toss until evenly coated. Place in air fryer basket and air-fry 15 to 18 minutes or until golden brown and tender, turning them twice during this time.

Test Kitchen Tip: *Although we give you a range for how long these should cook, please keep in mind that it may vary greatly based on how hard or ripe the plantains are. The riper the plantain, the sweeter and more tender, so don't try this with a yellow, unripe one! Otherwise, you might find yourself frustrated with less-than-tasty results.*

Cinnamon-Roasted Fall Veggies

Maybe you're not a fan of Brussels sprouts because you've only ever had 'em boiled and maybe the only way you've ever eaten squash is mashed and slathered with butter (not such a bad way, really!). If you've been nodding your head, then you're in for something really exciting. This side dish features some of our favorite fall flavors, including roasted squash (in the air fryer, of course!), Brussels sprouts, cranberries, cinnamon, and maple syrup. Yum!

Serves 4

Ingredients

2 tablespoons vegetable oil

½ teaspoon ground cinnamon

½ teaspoon salt

¼ teaspoon black pepper

2 cups cubed fresh butternut squash [see Tip]

8 ounces fresh Brussels sprouts, trimmed and cut in half

¼ cup dried cranberries

2 tablespoons maple syrup

Preparation

1   Preheat air fryer to 370 degrees F. In a large bowl, combine oil, cinnamon, salt, and pepper; mix well.

2   Add squash and Brussels sprouts and toss until evenly coated. Place vegetable mixture in air fryer basket.

3   Air-fry 5 minutes, turn vegetables over, and continue to cook 5 more minutes. Turn vegetables over again and continue to cook 4 to 5 minutes or until vegetables are tender and begin to brown.

4   Place in a large bowl and sprinkle with dried cranberries. Drizzle with syrup and toss gently. Serve immediately.

Test Kitchen Tip: *No need to struggle with cutting through a hard squash! You can just buy it pre-cut in the produce department or cubed in the freezer case. If you do buy them frozen, just add them to the Brussel sprouts a couple minutes later than what is suggested above, so they don't overcook.*

Bread Bowl Sage Stuffing

Here is how we suggest you serve this: pass it around the table and let everyone take a spoonful. Then pass it around again (because they're going to ask you to anyway!). Keep passing it around until it's all gone. Once it is, you can let everyone tear apart the edible bread bowl so they can use it to sop up any gravy left on their plates. (This is a great recipe for a weeknight or a holiday meal!)

Serves 5

Ingredients

1 (1-pound) 7-inch round mountain or sourdough bread (NOT sliced)

Cooking spray

½ stick butter

½ cup chopped onion

½ cup chopped celery

¾ cup chicken broth

¼ teaspoon ground sage

⅛ teaspoon black pepper

Preparation

1 Preheat air fryer to 380 degrees F. Cut about 1 inch off top of bread and set aside. Hollow out inside of bread, leaving about ¼-inch of bread around edges and on bottom; set aside. Cut top of bread and bread you've removed into ½-inch cubes.

2 Place bread cubes in a large bowl. Coat air fryer basket with cooking spray. Lightly spray bread cubes with cooking spray and toss to evenly coat. Place in basket and air-fry 6 minutes, shaking basket twice during cooking so that everything cooks evenly. Remove toasted bread cubes to a large bowl and set aside.

3 Meanwhile, in a medium skillet over medium heat, melt butter. Sauté onion and celery 5 to 7 minutes or until tender. Combine sautéed vegetables with toasted bread cubes, broth, sage, and pepper; mix well.

4 Preheat air fryer to 320 degrees F. Spoon stuffing mixture into bread bowl (see photo). Using a 4-inch-wide foil sling (see page ix), place bread bowl in basket and cook 15 minutes or until heated through and crispy on top.

Delectable Desserts

Blue Ribbon "Fried" Cookies

We just can't get enough of our favorite midway treats! (See our County Fair Fried Dough on page 270.) These look and taste like they are batter-dipped and deep-fried, but they're not! By making them in the air fryer, we save ourselves the extra calories and guilt. And unless you tell someone, they'll never be able to guess they aren't the real deal. Be generous with the powdered sugar and go to town!

Makes 10

Ingredients

1 (7.5-ounce) can refrigerated biscuits (10 biscuits)

¼ cup milk

10 chocolate sandwich cookies

Cooking spray

Confectioners' sugar for sprinkling

Preparation

1   Preheat air fryer to 320 degrees F.

2   Separate each biscuit in half. (Don't cut them in half, just separate the layers so you have 10 thinner biscuits.) Using your fingers, slightly flatten each piece so that it's bigger than a cookie.

3   Place milk in a small bowl, and quickly dunk a cookie in the milk. Place dipped cookie on a piece of dough and top with another piece of dough. Pinch edges together to seal and press dough gently around cookie. Repeat with remaining cookies and dough.

4   Coat air fryer basket with cooking spray. Lightly spray both sides of dough. Working in batches, if necessary, place in basket, making sure not to overcrowd. Air-fry 5 minutes or until golden. Repeat as needed with remaining cookies. Remove from basket, sprinkle heavily with confectioners' sugar, and serve.

Grandma's Classic Strawberry Shortcake

You don't need to put on your frilly apron or pull out the floral dinnerware to enjoy this classic dessert (but it sure would add a little extra charm!). These delightfully light and fluffy shortcakes are inspired by none other than grandma. Of course, back in the day, grandma didn't have an air fryer to make these easy-peasy. Fortunately for you, times have changed — now go on and enjoy this heavenly treat!

Makes 5

Ingredients

2 cups sliced strawberries

¼ cup granulated sugar

2 cups pancake and baking mix

⅓ cup lemon-lime soda

½ cup sour cream

2 cups frozen whipped topping, thawed

Confectioners' sugar for dusting

Preparation

1 In a small bowl, combine strawberries and granulated sugar. Cover and refrigerate at least 20 minutes to allow the mixture to create a simple syrup.

2 In a medium bowl, stir together baking mix, lemon-lime soda, and sour cream until mixture forms a dough. (The dough will be wet.) Turn dough out onto a lightly floured surface; knead 3 or 4 times or until dough comes together.

3 Using your hands, pat dough to a ¾-inch thickness. Using a 2-½-inch biscuit cutter, cut out 2 to 3 biscuits. Gather up the scraps and repeat the process until all dough is used up. Preheat air fryer to 370 degrees F.

4 Coat air fryer basket with cooking spray. Working in batches, place biscuits in basket, leaving at least ½-inch on all sides as the biscuits will expand during cooking. Air-fry 8 to 9 minutes or until fluffy and golden. Repeat with remaining biscuits. Let cool slightly on a wire rack.

5 To assemble strawberry shortcakes, split biscuits in half and place bottom halves on plates. Generously spoon whipped topping, then strawberries on each biscuit, reserving some of each for the tops. Place tops on biscuits and dust with confectioners' sugar. Dollop with reserved whipped topping, and spoon remaining strawberries over top.

Upside-Down Tropical Cake

Upside-down pineapple cakes are good, but we wanted to share something new that's even better. This twist on an old favorite features a from-scratch, carrot and coconut cake, as well as the iconic pineapple rings and cherries you love. And because this is made in a 6-inch cake pan, it's the perfect size!

Serves 3

Ingredients

- 1 tablespoon butter, melted
- 3 tablespoons brown sugar
- 3 slices canned pineapple, drained
- 3 maraschino cherries, drained
- ½ cup granulated sugar
- ½ cup all-purpose flour
- ½ teaspoon baking soda
- ¼ teaspoon ground cinnamon
- ¼ teaspoon salt
- 1 egg
- 2 tablespoons vegetable oil
- ½ cup grated carrots
- ¼ cup flaked coconut

Preparation

1 Coat a 6-inch baking pan (one that comes with your air fryer that's at least 2 inches deep or any one that fits in it) with cooking spray. Pour butter over bottom of baking pan, then sprinkle evenly with brown sugar. Place pineapple rings on top and a cherry in the center of each pineapple ring; set aside. Preheat air fryer to 320 degrees F.

2 In a large bowl with an electric mixer, beat remaining ingredients until well mixed. Pour batter over pineapple.

3 Place baking pan in air fryer basket and air-fry 25 to 27 minutes or until a toothpick inserted in center comes out clean. Let cool 5 minutes; loosen gently around the edges with a knife, then invert onto a platter. Let cool completely, then slice and enjoy.

Pound Cake "French Fries"

We're super proud of this recipe, as we think it does a darn good job of demonstrating that you don't have to get complicated to be creative. Look at the photo! Who would ever think that these "fries" started off with a frozen, store-bought pound cake? After we cut 'em, butter 'em, and toast 'em in the air fryer, they look like the real thing! This fun dessert will have everyone smiling.

Serves 10

Ingredients

⅓ cup granulated sugar

½ teaspoon ground cinnamon

1 (10.75-ounce) frozen pound cake, thawed

½ stick butter, melted

Preparation

1 In a medium bowl, combine sugar and cinnamon; mix well and set aside.

2 On a cutting board, cut pound cake into ½-inch slices. Lightly brush both sides of each slice with butter, then cut into ½-inch sticks, so they resemble french fries. Preheat air fryer to 350 degrees F.

3 Spray air fryer basket with cooking spray. Working in batches, if necessary, place pound cake "fries" in basket (overlapping a few is fine). Air-fry 3 minutes, turn "fries" over, and continue to cook 1 to 2 more minutes or until evenly toasted.

4 Toss "fries" in cinnamon-sugar mixture until evenly coated. Serve warm or at room temperature.

Serving Suggestion: *No, that isn't ketchup you see in the picture, but rather some strawberry jam that we warmed up slightly (or you can use ice cream topping) to use as the perfect dipping sauce.*

Magical Molten Lava Cakes

No matter how many times we've made lava cakes, they never cease to amaze us. How does the outside bake so perfectly and the inside remain so fudgy and gooey? There's definitely some kind of magic (aka chocolate science) happening there — and we're not complaining! You know what? It's not too important HOW it happens, so long as there's a decadent dessert to be enjoyed when it's done!

Makes 2

Ingredients

3 tablespoons butter

¼ cup semisweet chocolate chips

1 teaspoon self-rising flour

2 tablespoons sugar

½ teaspoon vanilla extract

1 large egg

1 large egg yolk

Preparation

1 Preheat air fryer to 350 degrees F. Coat 2 (1-cup) ramekins with cooking spray.

2 In a medium, microwave-safe bowl, microwave butter 1 minute or until melted. Add chocolate chips and whisk until completely melted and smooth.

3 Add flour, sugar, and vanilla to the chocolate mixture; mix well. Whisk in egg and yolk until smooth. Spoon batter evenly into ramekins and place in air fryer.

4 Air-fry 8 minutes or until cakes are just set and centers are soft. (Don't overcook or the molten center won't be molten.) Let sit 3 minutes to firm up slightly. While still warm, run a knife around the edge of each ramekin to loosen, then invert each onto a plate, and flip back over onto another plate so it's right side up. Serve warm.

Test Kitchen Tip: *This recipe is easy to double, just make sure you have room in your air fryer for more or cook them in batches.*

Bakery-Style Macaroons

To understand the perfect texture of a macaroon, you just have to try one of these. Honestly, we think we nailed this recipe. These coconutty-meringue favorites taste like they came straight out of a fancy bakery, and it's all thanks to the air fryer. To give these an even fancier look, we added a chocolate drizzle and a cherry on top. (Doesn't a cherry on top always make things better?)

Makes 18

Ingredients

1 (14-ounce) package sweetened, shredded coconut

3 large egg whites

¾ cup sugar

1 teaspoon almond extract

9 maraschino cherries, drained well and cut in half

½ cup semi-sweet chocolate chips

1 teaspoon shortening

Preparation

1 Place coconut in a large bowl; set aside.

2 In a medium saucepan over medium heat, combine egg whites and sugar. Cook 2 to 3 minutes or just until sugar has dissolved and mixture is bubbly, stirring occasionally. Remove from heat and stir in almond extract. Pour mixture over coconut; mix until well combined.

3 With your hands, squeeze together heaping tablespoons of coconut mixture, forming slightly rounded mounds. (They should be about the size of ping pong balls.) Place mounds on a baking sheet and press a cherry half on top of each one. Preheat air fryer to 310 degrees F.

4 Working in batches, place mounds in air fryer basket, making sure not to overcrowd. Air-fry 9 to 10 minutes or until macaroons are golden. Remove to a wire rack to let cool. Repeat with remaining macaroons.

5 Meanwhile, in a small microwave-safe bowl, microwave chocolate chips and shortening in 30 second intervals or until melted and smooth, stirring after each heating. Drizzle over macaroons.

Bite-Sized Pecan Pie Tarts

These are our "always-on-hand dessert." The reason is, you can bake these ahead of time and store them in the fridge or freezer. Then when unexpected company shows up, all you have to do is warm them up in the air fryer for about a minute or so. These bite-sized treats taste homemade and fresh every time. Put on a pot of coffee and enjoy a few sweet moments with company.

Makes 15

Ingredients

½ cup chopped pecans

½ cup packed light brown sugar

1 egg

1 teaspoon vanilla extract

1 tablespoon butter, melted

⅛ teaspoon salt

1 (1.9-ounce) package frozen mini phyllo shells

Preparation

1 Preheat air fryer to 300 degrees F.

2 In a medium bowl, combine pecans, brown sugar, egg, vanilla, butter, and salt; mix well. Spoon pecan mixture evenly into shells.

3 Coat air fryer basket with cooking spray. Place filled shells in basket and air-fry 6 to 7 minutes or until filling is firm. Cool slightly and remove to a wire rack to cool completely. Serve immediately or store in an airtight container until ready to serve.

Test Kitchen Tip: *No need to thaw the phyllo shells before filling and air frying them. It doesn't get any easier than this!*

Cookies & Cream Mini Cheesecakes

These are made with one of America's favorite cookies. You know, the ones that you dunk in milk, twist and eat the middle out of, and crumble on top of your ice cream. In this recipe, they make up the crust in our (perfectly-sized) mini cheesecakes. So if you can't decide between a cookie or a piece of really creamy cheesecake, no worries – you can have both in every forkful.

Makes 4

Ingredients

¾ cup finely crushed mini chocolate sandwich cookies

2 tablespoons butter, melted

12 ounces cream cheese, softened

½ cup sugar

2 eggs

½ teaspoon vanilla extract

¼ cup water

Whipped cream for garnish

4 mini chocolate sandwich cookies for garnish

Preparation

1 Lightly spray 4 (1-cup) ramekins with cooking spray.

2 In a small bowl, mix together cookie crumbs and butter. Place 2 tablespoons of crumb mixture in each ramekin and, using your fingers, press down crumbs to form a bottom crust. (We don't want the crust on the sides like a pie!) Preheat air fryer to 310 degrees F.

3 In a medium bowl with an electric mixer, beat cream cheese and sugar until smooth. Add eggs and vanilla; beat until creamy. Divide batter evenly between ramekins.

4 Pour water into air fryer pan. (This will create the perfect moist surroundings for these to bake in.) Working in batches, if necessary, place ramekins in air fryer basket and air-fry 11 to 12 minutes or until tops are firm and slightly jiggly in the center.

5 Let cool to room temperature, then refrigerate at least 4 hours or until ready to serve. You can serve these right out of the ramekins or if you would like to remove them, run a knife around the edge and invert them onto a plate. (Gentle shaking may be required.) Once they pop out, gently invert them right-side up. Garnish with whipped cream and mini chocolate sandwich cookies.

Easy Apple Hand Pies

This is one of our fastest dessert recipes, and that's just part of the reason why we love it so much. We also love them for how they look and how yummy they taste. Can you imagine the oohs and aahs you'll get when you bring these to the school bake sale? Or hey, maybe the next time your friends get together for a game, you can surprise them with these sweet treats!

Makes 8

Ingredients

1 egg

2 teaspoons water

1 (14.1-ounce) package refrigerated pie crusts (2 crusts)

1 (21-ounce) can apple pie filling (see Tip)

2 tablespoons coarse sugar

Preparation

1 Combine egg and water in a small bowl; set aside.

2 Roll out each crust into a 12-inch circle. Using a 3-inch apple-shaped cookie cutter, cut out 16 pieces of dough.

3 Place 1 tablespoon of pie filling in the center of 8 of the cut-outs. Brush edges around pie filling with egg mixture. Top with remaining dough. Using a fork, seal edges together. Brush tops of each hand pie with remaining egg mixture and sprinkle evenly with sugar. Preheat air fryer to 380 degrees F.

4 Coat air fryer basket with cooking spray. Working in batches, place hand pies in basket and air-fry 4 minutes. Turn over and continue to cook 3 more minutes or until golden. Repeat with remaining hand pies.

Test Kitchen Tip: *We love the convenience of apple pie filling; however, since these are hand pies, we suggest cutting the larger pieces of apple into smaller pieces, to ensure that every bite has some apple. Since we only use about half the can of pie filling for one batch, keep the rest in the fridge. That way you can make another batch in a few days. (Trust us, you'll want to!)*

County Fair Fried Dough

There are a few things you should always do if you're visiting a county fair. First, ride all the amusement rides you can handle. Second, play the carnival games (bonus points if you win a giant stuffed animal!). Finally, and most importantly, visit the food stands and get yourself some sugary-sweet fried dough. And if you can't make it to the fair this year, no problem. At least now you can recreate some of the fun at home!

Makes 4

Ingredients

⅓ cup sugar

1 pound store-bought pizza dough, kept at room temperature 30 to 60 minutes to let rise

Cooking spray

Preparation

1 Preheat air fryer to 400 degrees F. Place sugar in a shallow dish.

2 Place dough on a cutting board and cut into 4 quarters. Using your fingers, form dough into 6-inch circles. (You may want to dust your board and fingers with a bit of flour to prevent them from sticking.) Using a fork, prick dough about 10 times (to prevent it from bubbling up while baking). Lightly spray both sides of dough with cooking spray and dip both sides in sugar.

3 Coat air fryer basket with cooking spray. Place 1 piece of dough in basket and air-fry 3 minutes. Using tongs, turn over and continue to cook 2 to 3 more minutes or until light golden.

4 Remove "fried" dough and dip in remaining sugar, pressing firmly so sugar sticks to dough. Repeat process with remaining dough. After the last piece is "fried," place all pieces back in basket for 1 minute to warm up.

Campfire S'mores Stuffed Cupcakes

Your favorite campfire dessert, with no campfire required! These "bake" up in your air fryer and deliver a trio of yummy flavors. From the rich and fudgy cupcake stuffed with marshmallow crème, to the decadent chocolate frosting with graham cracker crumbles — these cupcakes are amazing. And if you're really missing that whole outdoor experience, you can always enjoy these under the stars.

Makes 4

Ingredients

½ cup all-purpose flour

¼ cup sugar

2 tablespoons cocoa powder

½ teaspoon baking soda

¼ teaspoon salt

¼ cup vegetable oil

¼ cup milk

½ teaspoon vanilla extract

4 tablespoons marshmallow crème

Chocolate frosting for topping (Store bought or homemade)

Coarsely chopped graham crackers for sprinkling

Preparation

1 Preheat air fryer to 310 degrees F. Place 4 cupcake liners in air fryer basket.

2 In a medium bowl, combine flour, sugar, cocoa powder, baking soda, and salt. Add oil, milk, and vanilla; mix well. Pour batter evenly into cupcake liners.

3 Air-fry 13 to 15 minutes or until a toothpick inserted in center comes out clean. Let cool.

4 Using an apple corer or teaspoon, make a small hole in the top of each cupcake. Fill each evenly with marshmallow crème. (This works best if you place the marshmallow crème in a plastic bag, snip the corner, and pipe in.) Top cupcakes with chocolate frosting and sprinkle with graham cracker pieces.

Hot 'n' Bubbly Blueberry Cobbler

It's nearly impossible to resist this dessert, especially when you can smell it coming fresh out of the … air fryer? Yep! We suggest getting this prepped and ready for cooking just before dinner. That way halfway through eating, you can pop it in your air fryer and within minutes, your house will be filled with the most incredible aroma ever. From our experience, no one leaves the dinner table to skip out on this dessert.

Serves 6

Ingredients

1 (21-ounce) can blueberry pie filling

1 cup fresh blueberries

Zest of 1 lemon

½ cup old-fashioned oats

¼ cup brown sugar

2 tablespoons all-purpose flour

3 tablespoons cold butter, cut into chunks

Preparation

1 Preheat air fryer to 320 degrees F.

2 In a 7-inch, deep-dish baking pan (the one that comes with your air fryer or any that fits in it) combine pie filling, blueberries, and lemon zest; mix well.

3 In a small bowl, combine oats, brown sugar, flour, and butter; mix until crumbly. Sprinkle crumb topping over blueberry mixture.

4 Air-fry 13 to 15 minutes or until golden and bubbly.

Serving Suggestion: *Just like cookies need milk and french fries need ketchup, any good fruit cobbler needs to be served up with a generous scoop of ice cream. So go to town … you have our permission.*

Peanut Butter Cup Wraparounds

Calling all peanut butter cup lovers! This dessert is just for you and it's so easy. With just five ingredients and in less than 15 minutes, you can be snacking on a sweet treat made with your favorite chocolate and peanut butter candy. These are practically guaranteed to make you smile, so we suggest you make them whenever you need a little pick-me-up!

Makes 8

Ingredients

1 (8-ounce) can refrigerated crescent rolls

8 miniature peanut butter cups

¼ cup semi-sweet chocolate chips

½ teaspoon shortening

2 tablespoons chopped peanuts

Preparation

1 Preheat air fryer to 350 degrees F.

2 Separate crescent dough into triangles. Place a peanut butter cup near the wide end of each triangle and roll dough up around peanut butter cup (the same way you would roll for crescent rolls), tucking sides underneath and pinching to seal.

3 Coat air fryer basket with cooking spray. Working in batches, if necessary, place wraparounds in basket, making sure not to overcrowd. (They will expand during cooking.) Air-fry 3 minutes. Turn over and continue to cook 1 more minute or until golden. Repeat with remaining wraparounds.

4 In a small microwave-safe bowl, microwave chocolate chips and shortening in 30 second intervals or until melted and smooth, stirring after each heating. Drizzle melted chocolate over wraparounds and sprinkle evenly with chopped peanuts.

Banana Split Croissants

We bet you've never had a banana split quite like this one! In this recipe, the air fryer is used to warm up stuffed croissants. Once everything is melty and gooey, top each one with your favorite sundae toppings. (As you can see, we've got quite a few.) Whether you serve yours as-is or with a scoop of ice cream, you're going to be in for a real treat!

Serves 4

Ingredients

4 mini bakery croissants, cut in half lengthwise

¼ cup chocolate hazelnut spread

2 bananas, cut in half lengthwise and then again crosswise

¼ cup strawberry ice cream topping

¼ cup pineapple ice cream topping

¼ cup frozen whipped topping, thawed

2 tablespoons chopped walnuts

4 maraschino cherries

Preparation

1 Preheat air fryer to 350 degrees F.

2 Place top and bottom of croissant on a cutting board and evenly spread 1 tablespoon chocolate hazelnut spread on the cut side of both pieces. Place 2 banana slices on bottom half of croissant and place top of croissant on banana slices. Repeat with remaining croissants, chocolate hazelnut spread, and bananas.

3 Place croissants in air fryer basket and air-fry 3 minutes or until toasted and chocolate hazelnut spread has melted.

4 Remove to serving plates and spoon 1 tablespoon each of strawberry and pineapple toppings on each croissant. Top each croissant with whipped topping, walnuts, and a cherry. Serve immediately.

Test Kitchen Tip: *You can find mini croissants in the freezer aisle or check out your grocery store's bakery.*

Nutty Baked Apples with Caramel Drizzle

Fresh apples and cozy comforting desserts seem to go hand-in-hand. So we took some fresh-from-the-orchard apples and stuffed them full of a warm-ya-up cobbler. The results ... well, you be the judge of that. In every yummy bite you'll get the crunch of a cobbler topping and the sweet gooeyness of caramel. If you pardon the pun, we think you're really going to "fall" for this one!

Makes 4

Ingredients

4 medium apples

¼ cup chopped walnuts

3 tablespoons instant oats

2 tablespoons brown sugar

¼ teaspoon ground cinnamon

⅛ teaspoon ground nutmeg

2 tablespoons butter, cut into small pieces

Caramel sauce for drizzling

Preparation

1 Preheat air fryer to 330 degrees F. Using an apple corer or paring knife, core each apple. (Make sure not to go through the bottom of the apple or the filling will come out.)

2 In a small bowl, combine walnuts, oats, brown sugar, cinnamon, nutmeg, and butter; mix until crumbly. Spoon nut mixture evenly into center of apples.

3 Coat air fryer basket with cooking spray. Place apples in basket and air-fry 10 to 15 minutes, depending on how soft you like your baked apples. Serve warm with a generous drizzle of caramel.

Chocolate Chunk Jumbo Cookies

Whether you need a little something for a last minute birthday party or you've got the hankerin' for a monster-sized chocolate chip cookie, with this recipe and a little help from your air fryer, you've got everything you need to deliver lots of smiles. The nice thing about this dough is that after you whip up a batch, you can keep it in your fridge for a few days and bake a fresh cookie in just minutes.

Makes 6

Ingredients

½ cup rolled oats

2-¼ cups all-purpose flour

1-½ teaspoons baking soda

1 teaspoon salt

¼ teaspoon ground cinnamon

2 sticks butter, softened

¾ cup packed brown sugar

¾ cup granulated sugar

1-½ teaspoons vanilla extract

2 eggs

1-½ cups semisweet chocolate chunks

¾ cup chopped walnuts

Preparation

1 In a food processor or blender, pulse oats until fine.

2 In a large bowl, combine oats with flour, baking soda, salt, and cinnamon.

3 In another large bowl with an electric mixer, cream together butter, both sugars, and vanilla. Add eggs and mix until smooth. Stir in oats mixture; mix well. Stir chocolate chunks and nuts into dough; mix well. Cover and refrigerate until ready to use.

4 Preheat air fryer to 300 degrees F. Line a 6-inch baking pan with parchment or wax paper. Working in batches, spoon 1 cup of dough into baking pan, spreading evenly.

5 Air-fry 18 to 20 minutes or until a toothpick inserted in center comes out clean. Let sit 5 minutes, then remove cookie to a wire rack to cool. Repeat with remaining dough. Remove parchment paper and serve.

Lemon Curd & Raspberry Bundles

This dessert scores high in the "light and refreshing" category. These little bundles feature a flaky puff pastry crust, a pucker-up delicious lemon curd filling, and a colorful pop of raspberry goodness. They're just the right amount of sweet and tart, and are sure to brighten up your day. How about inviting some friends over to share these with?

Makes 9

Ingredients

1 sheet frozen puff pastry (from a 17.3-ounce package)

1 egg

9 teaspoons lemon curd

9 fresh raspberries

Confectioners' sugar for sprinkling

Preparation

1 Thaw puff pastry sheet 30 minutes.

2 In a small bowl, whisk egg; set aside. Unfold pastry on a cutting board and cut into 9 equal squares. Place 1 teaspoon of lemon curd in center of each square. Place 1 raspberry on top of lemon curd. Brush edges with egg. Bring corners together, pinching seams together, and gently twist dough (creating a little bundle). Preheat air fryer to 380 degrees F.

3 Coat air fryer basket with cooking spray. Working in batches, if necessary, place bundles in basket, making sure not to overcrowd. (They will expand during cooking.) Air-fry 8 to 9 minutes or until golden. Repeat with remaining bundles. Let cool 10 minutes, then sprinkle with confectioners' sugar, and serve.

Chocolate-Dipped Buttery Shortbread

This recipe was actually adapted from an Old World recipe that Howard's grandmother passed on to him. We thought it'd be a fun challenge to make her classic shortbread in an air fryer. Turns out, it's totally doable and delicious! We're sure Grandma Rose would be very proud. To make these even more special, we dipped them in chocolate, just like she used to.

Makes 16

Ingredients

2 cups all-purpose flour

⅓ cup confectioners' sugar

⅛ teaspoon salt

¾ cup butter, softened

1 teaspoon vanilla extract

1-½ cups semisweet chocolate chips

Preparation

1 In a large bowl, combine flour, sugar, and salt; mix well. Add butter and vanilla, and mix until dough forms. (You may need to work the dough with your hands until it comes together.) Roll into a ball, cover, and refrigerate 30 minutes.

2 Preheat air fryer to 300 degrees F.

3 On a lightly floured, large cutting board, roll out dough to ¼-inch thickness. Cut into 1- x 3-inch pieces. (To give this the classic shortbread look, create shallow rows of dimples with a fork, as shown.) Working in batches, if necessary, place dough pieces in air fryer basket (dimples up) and air-fry 8 minutes or until edges are slightly golden. Remove cookies to wire racks and allow to cool. Repeat with remaining dough.

4 In a microwave-safe bowl, melt chocolate in microwave for 1 to 1-½ minutes or until chocolate is smooth, stirring occasionally. Dip cookies ⅓ of the way into chocolate and place on wax paper-lined platter. Let sit until chocolate hardens.

Recipes in Alphabetical Order

Recipes by Category

Recipes by Category

Recipes by Category

Recipes by Category

Recipes by Category

Recipes by Category

Recipes by Category

Notes